The Great Book of Ice Hockey

Interesting Facts and Sports Stories

Sports Trivia Vol.1

**Bill O'Neill
&
Ryan Black**

Copyright © 2017 by LAK Publishing

ALL RIGHTS RESERVED

No part of this book may be reproduced, stored in a retrieval system, or transmitted in any form or by any means, electronic, mechanical, photocopying, recording, scanning, or otherwise, without the prior written permission of the publisher.

ISBN: 978-1-64845-017-4

DON'T FORGET YOUR FREE BOOKS

GET THEM FOR FREE ON
WWW.TRIVIABILL.COM

Contents

Introduction 1
THE GAME 2
   An Ancient Game 2
The Tools of the Trade 6
It's the Law – Rules of the Game 10
It's Child's Play - Youth Hockey and the
Minors 15
     Canada 16
     United States 17
     Europe 17
Now It's Getting Serious - Juniors and Major
Juniors 20
     Canada 20
     United States 22
     American Athletic Union 23
     Europe 23
Scholars and Skaters - NCAA Hockey 25
Now You're Talking - Semi-Professional
Hockey (the Minor Pros) 28
The Big Time - the National Hockey League 33
     Early Days 34
     The Original Six 35

Post-Original Six Expansion 36
Have Union, Will Argue - the NHLPA and
Labor Disputes 39
   Labor Disputes 40
   Player Injury Lawsuit 41
Hockey Hardware – The Stanley Cup.....................43
Show Me the Hardware - NHL Awards..................46
The Shrine – The Hockey Hall of Fame 49
INTERNATIONAL HOCKEY....................................53
   The NHL's Greatest Rival – The KHL 53
Hockey Beneath the Midnight Sun – Liiga,
the Finnish Elite League 56
Sweden's Pride and Joy – The Swedish
Hockey League 59
   Head Coach and Union Buster – Jack
   Adams 62
"Coach Q" – Joel Quenneville.................................65
The Winningest Coach – Scotty Bowman 67
THE PLAYERS 70
The Great 8 – Alexander Ovechkin.........................70
Fabulous Number Four - Bobby Orr 75
The Greek God - Chris Chelios 79
"Mr. Hockey" - Gordie Howe 84
The Ageless Wonder - Jaromir Jagr 87
Super Mario - Mario Lemieux.................................91
The Devils' Own - Martin Brodeur 96

The Rocket - Maurice Richard 100
"Sid the Kid" – Sidney Crosby 103
"The Captain" Stevie Y - Steve Yzerman 108
The Finnish Flash - Teemu Selanne 112
The Uke - Terry Sawchuk 115
"The Great One" - Wayne Gretzky 119
ICE CHIPS 122
Girls Play, Too - Women's Hockey 122
Open Ice - Minorities in Hockey 125
Everyone Can Play - Para Ice Hockey 130

Don't Forget Your Free Books 133
More Books by Bill O'neill 134

Introduction

Ice hockey has some of the most devoted fans anywhere. They go to games, play in beer leagues, have fantasy leagues on the internet, teach their kids to play, cheer on their favorite players and spend millions of dollars annually on tickets and merchandising. The people involved with the game at every level are dedicated to this, their favorite sport.

Maybe you're one of these hockey fans. Maybe you're a player, or that special breed called a Hockey Mom. Maybe you've only recently become acquainted with the game through the prime-time television broadcasts of the Stanley Cup Playoffs. No matter your level of association with hockey might me, how much do you *really* know about the game?

This book is a look at the people and things that make ice hockey so great. Enjoy the facts presented here, and most of all, enjoy the game.

See you when the puck drops!

THE GAME

An Ancient Game

Ice hockey is believed to have arisen from stick-and-ball games that were played in prehistoric Europe. Some have even likened it to an early sort of game played in Ancient Egypt (obviously without ice). It is most closely related to the Irish game called hurling, and a Scottish game called "bandie ball," both of which were played with a stick and a ball on open fields. A similar game was described in the Icelandic sagas, indicating that a hockey-like game was played by the Norse.

The game was imported to the New World by soldiers and settlers from Great Britain. In Canada, the Mi'kmaq, a First Nations indigenous group, had their own versions of stick-and-ball games, often a sort of cross between hockey and lacrosse, and these games also became influential on the game of hockey. In the 1820s and 1830s, British soldiers frequently played on the ice and snow, and it was considered a "morning game". Players skated on the ice, nine men to a side, using hooked sticks and "bungs", or the corks out of whiskey barrels.

A version of hockey called "shinny" was played then, which had no actual rules, no goal tenders, and not even a set number of players to a side. It was as informal as it gets. The game as we know it today originated in Montreal, Canada, where the first organized indoor game was played by students from McGill University in March 1875 at Victoria Skating Rink. The rules were based on the rules of England's field hockey association, still using the word "ball," although instead of a ball, the players used a wooden disc, which was a precursor to the modern puck. The first hockey club, the McGill University Hockey Club, was founded in 1877, followed by the Quebec Bulldogs of the Quebec Hockey Club in 1878 and the Montreal Victorias, founded in 1881.

In 1880, the number of players on a side was reduced from nine to seven, and the number of teams continued to grow. In 1883, the first so-called "world championship" of ice hockey was played at the Montreal Winter Carnival. The trophy was called the Carnival Cup, and the first world champion was from McGill. In 1886, the teams that competed at the Montreal Winter Carnival organized the Amateur Hockey Association of Canada.

Hockey returned to its birthplace in Europe in 1885, when the Oxford University Hockey Club began to play. The first documented hockey rivalry arose in Europe during the first Ice Hockey Varsity Match, where the Oxford Dark Blue played against rival Cambridge in St. Moritz, Switzerland. Oxford won, and the rivalry continues to this day. There will be more about this under the "Rivalries" entry.

In 1888, the Governor-General of Canada, Lord Stanley Preston, attended a hockey game at the Montreal Winter Carnival at the behest of his sons and daughter, all of whom were hockey enthusiasts. He became a devotee of the sport, as well, and in 1892 he purchased a silver cup to recognize the best team in Canada. The Dominion Hockey Challenge Cup (later called the Stanley Cup) was first awarded in 1893 to the Montreal Hockey Club. Lord Stanley's son, Arthur Preston, organized the Ontario Hockey League, and his daughter Isobel was one of the first women to ever play the game.

Lord Stanley's five sons brought hockey back to England, playing a team made up of members of the royal court, including the future King George V, and defeating them in 1895 at Buckingham Palace. By 1903, hockey was being played in continental Europe, and the Ligue Internationale de Hockey Sur Glace was founded in 1908. Great Britain won the first European competition in 1910.

Hockey came to the United States for the first time in 1893, which was a banner year for hockey in general. The first "ice polo" game was played between Yale University and Johns Hopkins University. There were a hundred teams in Montreal alone, and leagues had been formed all throughout Canada, all the way west to Winnipeg, where goalie leg pads were used for the first time.

Professional hockey began in the early 20th century, starting with Western Pennsylvania Hockey League in 1902. In 1904, the league added teams in Michigan and Ontario to create the first ever fully professional league, the International Professional Hockey League. The International Ice Hockey Association was founded in 1906. In Europe, the first professional league was formed in Switzerland in 1912. The National Hockey League was founded in 1917, and hockey's first appearance as an Olympic sport was at the 1920 summer (yes, summer) Olympic Games in Antwerp, Belgium.

The rest, as they say, was history.

FUN FACTS:

1. The word "hockey" was first used in 1773 in the book *Juvenile Sports and Pastimes, to Which Are Prefixed, Memoirs of the Author: Including a New Mode of Infant Education* by Richard Johnson. Hockey was the sole subject of chapter eleven in the book.
2. Shinny is a term still used to describe street hockey and informal hockey. It is particularly popular in Nova Scotia.
3. The game was introduced to the States by an American financier, Malcolm Greene Chace.
4. The name for a hockey-like Viking game was *knattlikr*, and it has been played for over a thousand years. It is still played by re-enactors at colleges and medieval fairs.
5. "Hokie", a game played by throwing a ball with sticks, was outlawed in the 1573 Statute of Galway. This game was likely more related to lacrosse than to modern hockey.

The Tools of the Trade

Hockey is a full-contact sport where players wear knives on their feet and hit frozen vulcanized rubber discs as hard as they can while simultaneously wielding long clubs. Injuries are frequent and sometimes even fatal. To protect players, a number of changes have been made to the equipment used in the modern game. This is the gear that players need to play the game and survive.

Skates. Unlike figure skates, hockey skates are smooth and have a single edge from front to back. Goalie skates have shorter blades, which allows for better balance and for the side-to-side movement that is so necessary for the position. Skates should have strong ankle support and can sometimes come with extra hardened leather pieces to protect the feet and ankles from rogue pucks.

Helmet. The "brain bucket" part of a hockey helmet is virtually the same, no matter which of the three big manufacturers (Bauer, CCM and Warrior) made it. The variation comes with the accessories, which include full face visors, half-visors and face cages. In certain leagues, players are required to play with face cages. In the NHL, visors and the rest of the accessories are optional. Helmets are not. Goalie helmets are almost like the helmets worn by medieval knights. They are made of fiberglass and cover the entire head and jaw, with cages to protect the face. Most goalies customize the decoration on their helmets, ranging from the strictly utilitarian to the outlandishly colorful. Helmets are made of vinyl nitrate, which is supposed to redistribute the force of a blow from the point of contact. Helmets have liners made of polypropylene foam.

Stick. Hockey sticks used to be made of wood, usually ash, birch or willow. These lighter woods were preferred because they allowed for a certain amount of elasticity in the stick, which helps propel the puck faster on slapshots. Modern sticks are made of composite materials, usually carbon fibers and graphite. They are more elastic than the wooden sticks, but they seem to break very easily. Players create curves in the blades of their sticks, which helps with puck handling and shooting, and the degree of this curve is regulated in the rules.

Hockey Pants. Hockey pants run from waist to knee and are fully padded, with hardened plastic inserts to protect the hips and thighs from impacts. Additional pads can be purchased to add to the hockey pants, protecting the kidneys and lower back. Because they're usually quite loose, they are held up with suspenders.

Gloves. There are different gloves for different positions. The standard glove is padded on the top of the hand and fingers and thinner in the palm to allow better grip. Goalies have special gloves. One is called a blocker and one is the grabber. The blocker has a large, hard, paddle-shaped board that covers the wrist and hand, and it's used for blocking shots. The grabber is very much like a baseball glove and is used to catch pucks out of the air or to scoop them up off of the ice.

Shoulder Pads. This is sort of a misnomer, because the pads cover more than just the shoulders. They also protect the upper back, the chest, the ribs, shoulder blades and clavicles. The padding comes in varying thicknesses. The idea is to be protected from impacts and still have full range of motion, so proper fit is very important.

Elbow Pads. These are pads that are fitted via Velcro straps and which cover the elbows, triceps and forearms. Elbow pads are required in most leagues, because they're good protection in case of falls.

Shin Guards. These are absolutely vital, especially for players who intend to block shots or who get into hack-and-whack duels at the boards. These pads run from the kneecap to the top of the skate boot.

Neck Guard. These plastic guards are useful for all players, but especially for goalies. There have been some very horrifically bloody accidents involving throats and other players' skate blades. The neck guard is made of clear plastic and is suspended from the goalie's helmet with ties.

Jockstrap or Pelvic Protector. Self-explanatory.

Socks. These are colorful affairs that run from the ankle to the mid-thigh, and they attach to garter belts via Velcro tabs. Players frequently use to tape to keep their socks from slipping during play.

Jerseys. Also called "sweaters", these are the oversized shirts that have the team logo, the player's name and the player's number. They frequently have laces at the throat and scoop hems. In the NHL, players are required to have their jerseys tied down at all times. This is accomplished by means of something called a "fight strap," which attaches the jersey to the hockey pants.

FUN FACTS:

1. Helmets came into regular usage in 1933 after Ace Bailey, a player for the Toronto Maple Leafs, hit his head on the ice and nearly died. In fact, a priest at the arena gave him his last rites on the ice. Bailey survived, but his career was over.
2. Goalie Clint Malarchuk almost died on the ice when a Steve Tuttle's skate blade sliced his carotid artery and jugular vein. He lost over a liter of blood and needed 300 stitches to close the wound. Neck guards began to appear on goalies after that.
3. Goalies did not start wearing masks until 1959. Montreal Canadiens goalie Jacques Plante wore a mask in play for the first time after taking a shot to the face. He was reviled as a coward for wearing it.
4. Boston Bruins goaltender Gerry Cheevers used to draw stitches on his mask every time it got hit during a game.
5. **Bobby Orr was murder on sticks. He would go through 150 to 180 per season.**

It's the Law – Rules of the Game

There is not enough room in a book like this to appropriately address the rules of the game. There different rules for different leagues, and for different countries. Some of those rules are full of minutiae, like exactly how many inches wide a goalie's leg pads can be, and how much of an angle a shooter's stick blade can have. The basics, though, are as follows.

The game is played on a sheet of ice called the rink. In North America, the ice surface is 200 feet long and 85 feet wide. In Europe, the ice surface is somewhat larger, which can cause problems for players who are trying to transition from one system to the other. There is a red line crossing the rink width-wise at the exact center. There are two blue lines, one bisecting each half of the rink. These lines create the zones.

The goal nets are located in an area called the trapezoid, delineated by more lines in the ices, at either end of the rink. The zone containing a team's own goal is the defensive zone, because this is where the team will try to defend against a goal by their opponents. The other goal is in the offensive zone, because that's where the team is trying to score -

bringing the offense. The defensive and offensive zones are between the blue lines and the ends of the rink. The area in the center of the rink, between the blue lines, is called the neutral zone, because it's technically not "owned" by either team.

The puck is made of vulcanized rubber. It is one inch thick, three inches in diameter, and weighs about six ounces. When it's frozen, it's as hard as a rock. A player can move the puck with his stick, and sometimes with his foot, but it is forbidden for anyone but the goalie to pick up the puck with his hand.

The object of the game is to score more goals than the other team, which is to say, to get the puck past the other team's goaltender and into the net. The puck can be shot directly from the stick; it can be bounced in off of the goal net supports ("the pipes") or ricocheted off of another player. A player is not allowed to kick the puck into the net.

The hockey teams have one goaltender, three forwards and two defensemen (the "skaters") on the ice at all times, but the total number of players on a team is 22. That means four lines of three forwards each and three defensive pairs, plus the goaltender.

Players come and go from the bench at will, which is called "changing on the fly". Forwards go in as relief for winded forwards, and defensemen for defensemen. The players usually change as a unit, so three forwards (a line) come off and three forwards get in the game. The defensive pairs switch places, as well. Changing on the fly does not require a stoppage in play or the permission of the on-ice officials.

The goaltender can sometimes be pulled to the bench so that another skater can be added to the offensive push in an effort to score. This usually happens at the end of a close-scoring game. The problem with pulling a goaltender is that it leaves that team's net open and undefended, with frequently results in what's called empty-net goals. It's a risky move, but many coaches do it.

The game is played in three 20-minute periods. During any stoppage of play, the clock is stopped. Some leagues have overtime periods and shoot outs to determine a winner, in case the score is tied at the end of 60 minutes of play. Play starts with something called a faceoff, which is when the two teams' line up facing one another and the puck is dropped between them. The team for the player who wins the faceoff is said to have control of the puck. The opening faceoff takes place at center ice, but thereafter it takes place at different locations depending on what stopped the play before - offsides, icing, or a penalty.

There are four officials on the ice at all times, as well. There are two referees and two linesmen. The linesmen are responsible for determining whether a player has gone offside or committed icing. The referees are the ones who make all of the other calls, like charging, boarding, hooking, holding, and so forth. When a referee makes a call, he penalizes the offending player with time in the penalty box. A minor penalty is two minutes. A major is four minutes. During the course of the penalty, the offending player's team is shorthanded, and the team that is still at full strength is said to be on a power play. During their opponent's power play, the defending team is on a penalty kill, trying to keep the other team from scoring for the duration of the penalty. If the full strength team scores during a penalty, the penalty time is immediately cancelled and the offending player is returned to his team's bench. In hockey slang, he is said to be taking the skate of shame!

There other major penalties that happen frequently, and one of them is deeply beloved by hockey fans everywhere - fighting. If two players choose to fight each other ("have a go"), they will be penalized five minutes each. These are usually considered "offsetting penalties", meaning that neither team will be shorthanded and a substitution for the penalized player will immediately join the game. Egregious violations of the rules, including truly aggressive and obnoxious behavior like intending to cause injury to another player, can result in a misconduct, which results in a 10-minute visit to the penalty box, or a game misconduct, in which the offending player is ejected from the game entirely.

There are a whole host of specific rules, as mentioned before, but these are the major rules that any spectator needs to be aware of to understand the game.

FUN FACTS:

1. The pop musician who performs as Five for Fighting ("Superman") takes his stage name from the five-minute penalty for fighting.
2. Referees signal the penalties they're calling using hand signals. They also have microphones they can use to broadcast their decisions through arena loudspeakers.
3. A hockey player who starts a fight with another player as an obvious aggressor is called an instigator, and instigating is a minor penalty on its own.
4. The rules of NHL hockey are subject to change at the order of the NHL Board of Governors. The general managers of the various hockey clubs can offer insights and advice, but the Board of Governors has the final say.
5. There is an old saw about faceoffs: "If you're not cheating, you're not trying."

It's Child's Play - Youth Hockey and the Minors

Like with almost every pursuit that requires the constant development of skill and dedication to improvement, hockey usually demands that its players start early. This means that kids start playing in organized leagues before they're ten years old.

Skating can and does start sooner than this. Any number of pro hockey players' talk about starting on skates practically as soon as they can walk. Kids that young are too little for organized play, but they're not too small to develop a love of the game. Get them used to the old, to the ice, to the constant falling down, and they'll be ready for more. When they're ready for more, youth hockey will be waiting for them.

The two largest youth leagues are handled by USA Hockey and Canada Hockey. In youth hockey, because of the way humans develop, divisions are based on age. The names and the divisions depend upon which governing board is in charge of the youth league. There are also youth leagues in other countries, and we'll address those later.

Canada

The Canadian age groups are: Initiation (Mini-Mite), under 7; Novice (Mite), under 9; Atom (Squirt), under 11; Peewee, under 13; Bantam, under 15; Midget, under 18; and Juvenile, under 20, for those not going on to play at the Junior or Senior level. Juniors are for all players under 21, and it's divided into Junior C, Junior B, Junior A (which is the equivalent of Tier II hockey in the US), and Major Juniors, which is a competitive and semi-pro league. More on that later.

Canada Hockey has competitive and non-competitive divisions. The non-competitive rankings are House League (HL), Rostered Select, and League Select. HL consists of intra-city games, and players can be at any skill level. Rostered Select takes the best HL players and includes them in additional games on an ad hoc basis. League Select is the next step up, where it take the best HL players and has them play in a full season in a league in addition to their HL games.

The Canadian competitive system runs through the following tiers: House League, C, B, A, AA and AAA. In the competitive House League all games take place in the same league. 'C' level and above involves playing games with other associations across the region.

United States

In the United States, amateur youth hockey is overseen by USA Hockey, and the divisions are as follows:

Mite: under 8 (separated into Red, White and Blue divisions)

Squirt: ages 9 - 10 (Levels AA, A, B and C)

Peewee: ages 11 - 12 (Levels AAA, AA, A, B and C)

Bantam: ages 13-14 (Levels AAA, AA, A, B and C)

Midget Minor 15 and Under: age 15 - Level AAA

Midget Minor 16 and Under: ages 15-16 (Levels AAA, AA, Junior Varsity High School, High School A)

Junior: ages 16-20. More about Juniors later.

Europe

Youth hockey is played in Sweden, Finland, France, Germany and Switzerland.

In Sweden, the age-level divisions are: U9, U10, U11, U12, U13, U14, U15 and U16, which are administered by local leagues. At the age of 17, players fall under the purview of the Swedish Ice Hockey Federation, and they're divided up into two groups: Junior 18 and Junior 19.

For youth hockey in Finland, all teams are administered by the Finnish Ice Hockey Association, which divides its players into "school ages" and "under school ages". Players over 16 are considered Juniors. The youth hockey divisions are: G- and F-minors (under 11); E-minors (12-13); D-minors (14-15); C-juniors (16 and younger); B-juniors (18 and younger) and A-juniors (10 and younger).

French youth hockey has Moustiques (ages 9 and under); Poussins (ages 10-11); Benjamins (ages 12-13); Minimes (ages 14-15) and Cadets (ages 16-18). The governing body is the French Ice Hockey Federation.

German youth hockey divisions are Kleinstschüler (Bambini), ages 9 and younger;

Kleinstschüler, ages 11 and younger; Knaben, ages 13 and younger; Schüler, 15 and younger; Jugend, 17 and younger; and Junioren, 19 and younger. Designations and play are controlled by the German Ice Hockey Federation.

Last but not least, Swiss Junior Hockey has the following divisions: Bambini (ages 6-9 - there are two categories of Bambini, called Bambi and Bini); Piccolo (ages 11 and under); Moskitos (ages 10-12, with categories Moskitos B, A and Top); Mini (ages 12-14, with categories Minis B, A and Top); and Novizen/Novices/Novizi (ages 15-17, with categories Novices A, Top and Elite). Then they have the Juniors, who are ages 17-20, with categories Juniors A, Top, Elite B and Elite A. The Swiss Ice Hockey Federation is in charge here.

So, that's a lot of kids playing a lot of hockey.

FUN FACTS:

1. The NHL on NBC used to broadcast photographs of NHL players as children in youth hockey as part of a segment called "Name That Squirt."
2. At the Canadian Initiate level, players were once called "Tykes".
3. AAA level youth hockey is considered to be elite level competition.
4. Orillia, Ontario, population 30,000, has seven skill divisions for seven-year-olds.
5. In British Columbia, BC Hockey has a different set of divisions for competitive games.

Now It's Getting Serious - Juniors and Major Juniors

Junior hockey is a big deal. It involves players from the ages of 16 to 21, when pro careers are beginning to be seriously contemplated. To this end, professional and collegiate scouts start showing up at rinks, and money starts to change hands at the higher competitive levels of this category. For the purposes of this book, we will focus on the junior hockey systems in just two countries, Canada and the United States.

Canada

The junior leagues in Canada range from the purely amateur to the semi-pro. These divisions, from lowest to highest, are: Junior C and Junior B (Junior A in Quebec); Junior A (Junior AA in Quebec); and Major Juniors.

Junior C teams are essentially farm teams for the Junior B division, but they're still primarily locally-affiliated affairs. In Ontario, the Junior C division teams play every year for the Clarence Schmalz Cup.

Junior B teams compete in regional leagues, for regional trophies (the Sutherland Cup in southern Ontario, the Carson Trophy in Ottawa, the Coupe Dodge in Quebec, the Don Johnson Cup in the Atlantic Provinces, and the Keystone Cup in Western Canada). Talented Junior B players feed upstream to the Junior A.

The competition in Junior A is overseen by the Canadian Hockey League, the first time that a national body has gotten directly involved. Their annual trophy is the Royal Bank Cup, and successful and talented skaters move up to the Major Juniors.

Major Juniors is where everything changes. At this level, the NCAA considers players to be professional and therefore ineligible to play for colleges and universities in the United States. Players are paid a stipend and are allowed to sign entry-level contracts with NHL teams. They are in three different leagues: the Ontario Hockey League, which as 21 teams in Ontario, Michigan and Pennsylvania; the Western Hockey League, with 22 teams in the western Canadian provinces, Washington and Oregon; and the Quebec Major Junior Hockey League, which has 18 teams from Quebec and the Atlantic provinces. The QMJHL league trophy is called the President's Cup, not to be confused with the NHL award of the same name. In the OHL, they play for the J. Ross Robertson Cup. The WHL plays for the Ed Chynoweth Cup. The winners of the three major junior leagues then compete against each other for the Memorial Cup.

United States

In the United States, junior hockey is divided into three tiers.

In Tier III, there are eight sanctioned leagues: the Eastern Hockey League (EHL) Premier Division, the EHL 19U Elite Division, the North American 3 Atlantic Hockey League, the North American 3 Hockey League, the Rocky Mountain Hockey League, and the US Premier Hockey League, with has three divisions, Premier, Elite, and USP3. Players at this level are still amateur and often go on to compete at NCAA schools. At this level, players must pay a fee of between $4000 and $9,500 to cover the cost of room, board, and equipment, which the teams handle one the fees are collected. Most Tier III players are trying to move up to Tier II.

In Tier II, there is only one league, the North American Hockey League. Player expenses like room and board are not paid by the teams. The NAHL has 24 teams and they play each year for the Robertson Cup.

Tier I hockey has only one league, the United States Hockey League (USHL), and this is considered a professional level. Players who wish to play in college must complete their NCAA careers before playing here. There is no equipment fee, and the players' expenses are paid by the teams. There are two annual trophies in the USHL - the Clark Cup, for the winner of the playoffs, and the Anderson Cup, given to the team with the most points at the end of the regular season. There are 17 teams in this division.

American Athletic Union

The AAU split off from USA Hockey and started its own junior hockey league in 2011. In 2012, they renamed themselves the United Hockey Union. The claim to fame of this group is that it allows more foreign players (those born in countries outside of North America) than the other groups, with up to 14 non-North American players allowed per team, as compared to 4 per team in USA Hockey's Tier I division. The UHU has five different leagues: the National Collegiate Hockey Association, which is a college-level competitive league; the Central One Hockey League, which is Tier I Juniors; the Western States Hockey League, which is Tier II Juniors; the Canadian Premier Junior Hockey League, which is Tier III Juniors; and the National College Prospects Hockey League, which is Tier III Juniors.

Europe

In Europe, most junior level teams are affiliated with professional clubs, which use them as farm teams and development incubators for young talent.

FUN FACTS:

1. The average player's salary in the USHL is $58,680.
2. The Greater Metro Junior A Hockey League is an independent development league with teams drawn primarily from the metropolitan Toronto area.

3. The Manitoba Major Junior Hockey League is an independent league in the Winnipeg area. It is affiliated with Hockey Manitoba.
4. Gordie Howe played in the USHL with the Omaha Knights.
5. In the QMJHL, OHL and WHL, players earn an average of $500 a week.

Scholars and Skaters
- NCAA Hockey

The National Collegiate Athletic Association has two levels of play: Division I and Division III. Each division plays for its own championship. Division II championships were discontinued because of a lack of support for ice hockey in the Division.

Division I teams are considered the highest level in collegiate men's ice hockey competition, and the semi-finals and finals are branded as the Frozen Four. The school with the most NCAA Frozen Four championships is the University of Michigan, with nine victories. The Michigan Wolverines play for the Big Ten under the leadership of head coach Red Berenson, who has been behind the bench for a staggering 32 years. The traditional rival for the Wolverines is, of course, the Michigan State Spartans, and since 1990, these two teams have played at Joe Louis Arena in the Great Lakes Invitational. They have also played outdoor games, beginning with the game called "the Cold War" in 2001.

The Division III Championships have been played since 1984. The most successful Division III team in history is the Middlebury Panthers from Middlebury College in Vermont, who have skated to the title eight times.

As with all other sports in the NCAA, schools are assigned to divisions based upon how many different sports teams the schools promote for both genders. Division I schools must have at least seven different sports for both men and women with at least two team sports for each gender. Division II must have at least five sports, with two team sports for each gender. In Division III, there must be five sports and two team sports per gender. Further divisional differentiations are based on attendance, participation minimums, and financial aid requirements and prohibitions.

In women's hockey, the NCAA has teams in Division I only, with the first women's NCAA championship held in 2001, although many schools have had women's teams dating all the way back to the 1970's. Varsity women's hockey is played in 35 teams throughout the United States with a 30-game season, followed by an 8-team playoff bracket. The most women's NCAA Ice Hockey Championships have been won by the Minnesota Golden Gophers, with a total of six wins.

FUN FACTS:

1. In the 2013-14 NHL season, a whopping 31% of the NHL players in action had also played in the NCAA.
2. The NCAA has supplied more players to the

NHL than all of the countries in Europe combined.
3. Prior to the International Olympic Committee's decision to allow professionals to play for the gold medal, the majority of players on Team USA came from the NCAA.
4. NHL players with NCAA experience include goalie Jonathan Quick, All-Star forward Phil Kessel, Brooks Orpik and Kevin Shattenkirk.
5. Three Chicago Blackhawks players who also played for Team Canada in the 2014 Sochi Olympic Games were also NCAA alumni: Jonathan Toews, Duncan Keith and Patrick Sharp. (Chris Kunitz was the other NCAA alumnus on Team Canada that year.)

Now You're Talking - Semi-Professional Hockey (the Minor Pros)

Because hockey loves its hierarchies, there are three levels of minor professional league in North America. The AA and AAA leagues were established as the farm system for the NHL under the terms of the NHL Collective Bargaining Agreement. In this system, the teams in these minor leagues are affiliated with NHL teams, and their players are carefully drafted or scouted by the NHL teams with an eye toward someday developing into true professional-level players. Players in these leagues are represented by the Professional Hockey Players' Association (PHPA), a union with limited contract bargaining powers.

The "A" level minor hockey leagues are the Federal Hockey League (FHL), the Lige Nord-Américaine de Hockey (LNAH), and the Southern Professional Hockey League (SPHL). They are not considered in the NHL Collective Bargaining Agreement, and their players are not represented by the PHPA.

The "AA" level minor hockey league is the ECHL

(formerly the East Coast Hockey League), and its players feed into the AHL and sometimes, rarely, directly into the NHL. Players at the ECHL level generally have standard contracts, in which the player is signed by the affiliated NHL team but assigned exclusively to the minor league, or two-way contracts, in which players are signed by the NHL team and can go up and down the levels in the course of the season. Most ECHL contracts are standard contracts.

The "AAA" level minor hockey league, and the one just before "The Show" (the NHL) is the American Hockey League (AHL). Again, these players are signed by the parent team to either standard contracts or two-way contracts.

"A" Tier

The FHL only dates back to 2010. It is small, with only 7 teams in the Midwest and Northeastern United States, with one additional team located in Ontario. It is headquartered in Syracuse, New York. Its players go on to play in the ECHL, AHL and in Europe. Their annual championship trophy is called the Commissioner's Cup. The average FHL player earns $297.06 per week plus room and board during the season.

The LNAH was founded in 1996 as the Quebec Semi-Pro Hockey League, with its headquarters in - you guessed it - Quebec. It became a fully professional league in 2004. It is the lowest of the three "A" tier leagues in terms of skill, and most of its players seem to be of the brawling variety. At one point, the LNAH was averaging 3.2 fights per game. In the same time period, the NHL had less than one fight per game. The LNAH is also a home for declining NHL and AHL stars, and there is no limit to the number of veterans who can play for a team. There are 7 teams in the LNAH, and they play annually for the Futura Cup. The pay for the LNAH averages around $150 to $400 per week plus room and board during the season.

The SPHL was founded in 2004, and it has 10 teams in the southern United States. Its head office is in Huntsville, North Carolina. It has no teams in Canada, and the farthest north that the league extends is Evansville, Indiana. They play for the President's Cup. Their weekly salary is $100 to $300 plus room and board during the season.

"AA" Tier

The ECHL has 27 teams and is based out of Princeton, New Jersey. The league itself was first founded in 1988. Because the league is geographically spread out all over hither and yon, and because team owners complain about the cost of travel, there are some very stilted divisions and cross-divisional play is rare. The playoffs are arranged creatively, but always with a strange distribution of teams across divisions. There is only one ECHL team in Canada, with the rest of the teams located in the United States from the eastern seaboard to Idaho. Their trophy is called the Kelly Cup. Players at this level earn between $600 to $1000 a week, plus room and board during the season.

"AAA" Tier

This is where you find the royalty of the minor pro leagues, the AHL. Many players in the AHL system are on two-way contracts, and there is a lot of movement between the AHL and its big brother the NHL. The AHL was founded in 1936, with its headquarters in Springfield, Massachusetts. AHL salaries are set at a minimum of $42,375 but the average annual salary is around $68,000. The annual trophy for the AHL is the Calder Cup.

FUN FACTS:

1. In 2014, two FHL players (Jesse Felten of the Dayton Demonz and Matt Puntureri of the Danville Dashers) squared off at center ice. They proceeded to hug it out instead of throwing punches, and Puntureri pulled a can of beer out of his pants and shared it with his "opponent", toasting the crowd. It was the last game of the season for Danville, just before Dayton went on to the playoffs. The league was not amused. Because his season was essentially over, there was no discipline for Puntureri, but Felten was suspended for the remainder of the season and for the playoffs. Neither men played professionally in 2015, and while Felten has since returned to professional hockey with the Demonz, Puntereri is now playing in Germany.
2. Micheal Nylander and Patrick Rissmiller were two of the highest-paid AHL players ever, with each of them inking $1,000,000 salaries in the

2010 season.
3. The winningest team in the AHL is the Hershey Bears, who have earned the Calder Cup 11 times since the team's inception in 1938.
4. Injured NHL players are frequently sent to their team's AHL counterparts for "conditioning stints" (i.e., the chance to play their way back into game shape).
5. There is an active Facebook page called "Get Dayton Out of the FHL", which states that it is a "page dedicated to fans who would like to see a better fate and future for hockey in Dayton - or anywhere else suffering the Federal Hockey League". Harsh.

The Big Time - the National Hockey League

The Big Time. The Show. The Dance. Whatever you want to call it, the National Hockey League is *the* pre-eminent organization in the sport of ice hockey in North America, and arguably in the world. There are major professional leagues elsewhere on the planet, but most the top players there want to play in the NHL.

The NHL was founded on November 27, 1917, and it now has 30 teams, 23 in the United States and 7 in Canada. The league headquarters is in New York City, New York, and the commissioner is Gary Bettman. The league itself is ruled by the Board of Governors, which meets twice a year, once in June and once in December. The annual trophy for the league is the Stanley Cup.

There are two conferences with two divisions each. The Eastern Conference has the Atlantic Division and the Metropolitan Division. The Western Conference has the Pacific and Central Divisions. The league structure has changed many times over its years in existence, and the current format was finalized in time for the 2013-14 season.

Each NHL game has 60 minutes of play, with two 20-minute intermissions. If the game is tied at the end of regulation, then the teams play a five-minute four-on-four sudden death overtime period. If the teams are still tied, then there is a five-minute three-on-three sudden death overtime period. If the score remains unbroken at that time, then the game goes to a shootout. In the playoffs, instead of going to the four-on-four, the teams play 20-minute sudden-death overtime periods.

The regular season in the NHL consists of 82 round-robin games followed by a best-of-seven elimination tournament involving the first through sixth seeded teams in both conferences. The Western Conference Champions and the Eastern Conference Champions meet in the Stanley Cup Finals to play for the NHL's highest honor.

Early Days

Prior to the foundation of the NHL, the professional hockey league in North America was called the NHA, the National Hockey Association. The NHA started with six teams in Quebec and Ontario, but due to extremely acrimonious disputes with the owner of the Toronto Blueshirts, Eddie Livingstone, the rest of the owners in the league voted to disband in an effort to just get rid of the man. They reformed the following year as the NHL. In those days, the Stanley Cup did not exclusively belong to the NHL; indeed, at the time, it was an interleague championship involving teams in the NHL, the Pacific Coast Hockey Association, and the Western Canada Hockey League. The PCHA folded in 1924, and the WCHL in 1926.

The NHL expanded in the 1920s, and the Boston Bruins became the first American team in the league. World events conspired against professional hockey, from the international Spanish Flu pandemic in 1918 to the Depression to World War II. In 1942, many teams permanently shuttered their doors because there just weren't enough men left to play - they had all joined the Armed Forces of their respective countries and were overseas at war.

The Original Six

In 1942, the NHL was reduced to only six teams, which became known as the Original Six. These teams were: the Boston Bruins, the Chicago Blackhawks, the Detroit Red Wings, the Montreal Canadiens, the New York Rangers, and the Toronto Maple Leafs. All of these teams are still alive and kicking today, and they are arguably the most valuable teams in professional hockey...and they are certainly the most lucrative.

In 1947, the NHL took full control of the Stanley Cup.

Post-Original Six Expansion

With the advent of televised games in the mid-1960s, the league began to expand again. In 1967, the league doubled the number of its teams, adding the Los Angeles Kings the Minnesota North Stars, the Philadelphia Flyers, the Pittsburgh Penguins, the California Seals and the St. Louis Blues. In 1970, they added the Vancouver Canucks and the Buffalo Sabres. In 1974, these teams were joined by the Washington Capitals and the Kansas City Scouts.

The NHL was not the only game in town at this juncture, and a rival league called the World Hockey Association arose. In one season alone, 1972-73, the NHL lost 67 players to the WHA, including star Bobby Hull, whose contract with the WHA was the richest salary in hockey history at that time. The NHL tried to keep the WHA from poaching its talent by taking them to court, and the WHA countersued. The legal battles that followed devastated both leagues to the point that in 1979, the NHL and the WHA agreed to merge. The WHA ceased operations and the NHL absorbed four WHA teams, the Winnipeg Jets, the Edmonton Oilers, the Hartford Whalers and the Quebec Nordiques. The merger was initially blocked by a vote of team owners, losing by one vote, but a fan boycott of Molson beer created enough financial pressure on the owners of the Montreal Canadiens and the Vancouver Canucks to agree to the merger after all. Money talks.

In the 1990s, yet more teams joined the league. These were the San Jose Sharks, the Tampa Bay Lightning, the Ottawa Senators, the Mighty Ducks of Anaheim, the Florida Panthers, the Nashville Predators, and the Atlanta Thrashers. 2000 brought the Minnesota Wild and the Columbus Blue Jackets. The Winnipeg Jets were purchased and moved to Arizona in 1995, becoming the Phoenix Coyotes (now the Arizona Coyotes). In 1997, the Hartford Whalers moved south and became the Carolina Hurricanes. In 2011, in the most recent relocation, the Atlanta Thrashers moved to Winnipeg and were renamed the Jets in honor of the prior NHL team that had been in that city. In 2017, a new team, the Las Vegas Golden Knights, will begin play in the desert. When the Knights begin play, there will be 31 teams in the league. A 32nd is likely to follow, just to keep things even across conferences.

FUN FACTS:

1. The Hockey Hall of Fame is located in Toronto, Canada and is the permanent home to the Stanley Cup and the hardware for the major NHL awards. The entrance to the HOF is through the basement level of Eaton Mall.
2. Players in the NHL come from 19 different nations. The top six, in descending order by number: Canada, USA, Sweden, the Czech Republic, Russia, and Finland.
3. Player injuries are a constant concern, especially regarding concussions, which have ended some careers and severely impacted one of the NHL's biggest stars, Sidney Crosby.
4. The NHL Draft is a seven-round draft held every

June. Players from Europe, college, and junior hockey teams can enroll in the Entry Draft. Draft order is determined by the team's placement in the season just ending, so that the worst team in the NHL ("the cellar dweller") has the first pick and the Stanley Cup champions pick last. Each draft features a lot of wheeling and dealing behind the scenes, where team general managers trade players and draft picks.
5. Despite the fact that the NHL is the smallest of the four major professional sports leagues, it boasts the more affluent fan base, which in recent studies is said to be even richer than the fan base for the PGA.

Have Union, Will Argue - the NHLPA and Labor Disputes

The National Hockey League Players' Association is the labor union for the players. The union was created in 1967. The purpose of the NHLPA is to negotiate fair working conditions and equitable contract terms for players, and to enforce those terms and conditions, usually in opposition to the wishes of the team owners. The union also represents retired players.

Every team elects a Club Player Representative and an Alternate Club Player Representative to serve as voting members of the NHLPA Executive Board. The executive director of the union is a non-voting member of the board.

The first NHLPA was formed by Ted Lindsay of the Detroit Red Wings and Doug Harvey of the Montreal Canadiens. The union was formed to try to force the league's owners to release pension plan financial information. The owners successfully waged a union-busting campaign that made the NHLPA in its first incarnation to disband.

In 1967, the NHLPA reformed and sought recognition through the Canadian Labour Relations Board, seeking to avoid the fate of its predecessor. This time, the owners went along with the program, and the NHLPA has been a functioning body ever since.

Labor Disputes

There have been four work stoppages since the NHLPA began to operate:

The first strike only lasted for ten games in 1992, which were quickly rescheduled. This was as mild as labor disputes can get.

The second lockout was at the beginning of the 1994-5 season, and it resulted in the cancellation of the first half of the season. This lockout resulted in the CBA (collective bargaining agreement) that lasted until 2004.

The third lockout happened when the CBA expired and Gary Bettman, the NHL Commissioner, ordered a lockout of players until the NHLPA agreed to his terms. Strangely, this move made Mr. Bettman unpopular with players and fans alike. The lockout lasted for 310 days, which was the longest in professional sports history, and ended with the players being forced to accept a salary cap arrangement. The NHL lost its entire 2005-06 season, but Bettman got what he wanted and walked away with a new CBA with very favorable terms for the owners and the league.

The fourth lockout was in 2012, when the new CBA was negotiated with a clause reducing players' share of hockey-related revenues to less than 50%. These revenues included the use of players' names and likenesses. The league again canceled play until the new agreement was reached, but play resumed in January 2013. Again, the league got more or less what it wanted.

Player Injury Lawsuit

In 2013, just after the NFL paid out a settlement of over $700 million to injured players, ten former NHL players sued the NHL for failing to protect players from closed head injuries. The outcome of this suit is not yet known, as litigation is continuing. The NHLPA and the NHL have agreed upon a "concussion protocol."

FUN FACTS:

1. Due to the part he played in the third lockout, fans have taken great delight in vilifying Commissioner Gary Bettman since 2005. It is more or less tradition at this point to boo him as loudly as possible whenever he addresses arenas full of spectators. His fan name is "Buttman." You could say he's unpopular.
2. Past executive directors of the NHLPA include playing greats Ken Dryden, Phil Esposito and Bryan Trottier.
3. The NHLPA and NHL cooperate with the charitable cause Hockey Fights Cancer.

4. The NHLPA also operates NHPLA Goals and Dreams, which provides equipment and support to local hockey programs in 33 different countries, including in some Canadian First Nations communities.
5. The NHLPA recognizes the individual charitable efforts of its member players, including James van Riemsdyk's efforts on behalf of autism charities, Eric Lindros' fundraising for the Easter Seals, and programs in support of military veterans and their families.

Hockey Hardware
– The Stanley Cup

The NHL plays every year for the Stanley Cup, arguably the hardest trophy to win in all of professional sports. The cup was originally purchased and is therefore named for Lord Frederick Stanley, 16th Earl of Derby, also known as Lord Stanley of Preston. Lord Stanley was one of the original inductees into the Hockey Hall of Fame.

There are actually three Stanley Cups. The first is the Dominion Hockey Challenge Cup, meaning the cup at the very top of the modern trophy; the Presentation Cup, which is a certified original and travels with its very own Cup Keepers and is presented to winners at the end of every playoff series; and the Replica Cup, which resides in the Hockey Hall of Fame throughout the year.

The trophy is dominated by silver bands on which are etched the names of the winning teams, owners, coaches, players and support staff personnel. Every year, the new winners are added to the cup, and to keep the trophy a manageable size, silver bands are retired from oldest to newest as they fill up. The trophy is still etched by hand.

There are traditions about the Cup. At the end of the playoffs, the Cup is presented by the Commissioner to the Captain of the winning team. The captain is the first to hoist the cup above his head, and he then hands it off to his team mates until everyone has had the chance for a victory skate.

Other traditions include the belief that active players may only touch the Cup if they have won it - therefore, any NHL player who has not yet earned the honor may not touch the cup or drink out of it. Every year, winning players get to spend two days with the Cup, doing anything they want with it. This usually involves eating various foods, drinking a lot of alcohol, sleeping with it, taking it boating, or taking it to visit hospitals and sick kids. Some players have had their children baptized out of the Cup.

The Cup has a permanent escort of four "keepers", all of them employees of the Hockey Hall of Fame, but for the last sixteen years, the primary Cup Keeper has been Canadian Mike Bolt. Bolt has become a known face in his own right and once appeared in a series of credit card commercials.

FUN FACTS:

1. In 2008, Detroit Red Wings forward Kris Draper's infant daughter defecated in the Stanley Cup. (That wasn't intentional... Babies are babies, and it was a long photo shoot, and, well...)
2. The Stanley Cup weighs 15.5 kg, or 34.5 lbs. It stands 35.25 inches tall.

3. The Cup has its own Facebook page, with over 100,000 followers.
4. In May 2007, the NHL and seventeen former NHL players took the Cup to Kandahar in Afghanistan, where they played ball hockey with members of the Canadian armed forces, who were each allowed to drink from the cup, as well. The Cup has since made two more trips to Middle Eastern conflict zones.
5. In 2011, Cup Keeper Mike Bolt suffered a car breakdown while traveling in Quebec City, and he ended up hitchhiking with the Cup in tow. He's lucky Canadians more or less feel the Cup is sacred - if it had been stolen, the silver in the Cup is worth over $20,000.

Show Me the Hardware - NHL Awards

Every season, the NHL gives out awards to teams as well as on an individual basis. Some are given in accordance with statistical achievements, and others, which are not as easily and directly quantifiable, are voted on by the team general managers and/or the Professional Hockey Writers' Association. The individual awards and the performances they acknowledge are listed below.

Team Awards:

The Prince of Wales Trophy: Eastern Conference Champions

Clarence S. Campbell Bowl: Western Conference Champions

President's Trophy: Regular season champions

Individual Awards:

Hart Memorial Trophy: League MVP

Lady Byng Memorial Trophy: awarded to the player showing the best combination of outstanding sportsmanship, gentlemanly conduct and high standard of play (in actual practice: best player with the lowest penalty minutes)

Vezina Trophy: best goaltender

Calder Memorial Trophy: most outstanding rookie

Art Ross Trophy: most points in the season

James Norris Memorial Trophy: most outstanding defenseman (in actual practice: the defenseman who scores the most goals)

Conn Smythe Trophy: playoff MVP

Bill Masterton Memorial Trophy: the player displaying the most perseverance, sportsmanship and dedication to the sport of hockey (in actual practice, it usually goes to a player who returns to the game after suffering cancer or a personal tragedy)

Ted Lindsay Trophy: most outstanding player (elected by the NHLPA)

Jack Adams Award: best head coach

Frank J. Selke Trophy: the best defensive forward

William M. Jennings Award: the goaltender(s) with the best goals against average

King Clancy Memorial Trophy: the player demonstrating the most humanitarianism and leadership on and off the ice

NHL Foundation Award: the player who has done the most to enrich his community

Maurice "Rocket" Richard Trophy: top goal scorer

Roger Crozier "Saving Grace" Award: the goaltender(s) with the highest save percentage

Mark Messier Leadership Award: the player who shows the most leadership on and off the ice

NHL General Manager of the Year Award: self-explanatory

E. J. McGuire Award of Excellence: given to the draft prospect who best exemplifies commitment to excellence, strength of character, competitiveness and athleticism (elected by the NHL Central Scouting Unit)

FUN FACTS:

1. The Rocket Richard Trophy has been won by Alex Ovechkin a total of six times, and he has won the last four in a row. Nobody else has ever won this trophy more times.
2. The Norris Trophy was won by Bobby Orr for a record eight years.
3. The Selke Award was won in four consecutive years by Bob Gainey of the Montreal Canadiens, a league record.
4. Mario Lemieux of the Pittsburgh Penguins was the only player to ever win back-to-back Conn Smythe Trophies.
5. The Art Ross Trophy was won a staggering ten times, seven consecutively, by "The Great One," Wayne Gretzky.

The Shrine – The Hockey Hall of Fame

The Hockey Hall of Fame was established in 1943 by James T. Sutherland, the former president of the Canadian Amateur Hockey Association, in Kingston, Ontario, Canada, the putative "birthplace" of hockey. The first group of honorees were inducted in 1945 and included such luminaries as Hobey Baker, Georges Vézina and Howie Morenz.

The hall was moved to Toronto in 1958 after the NHL removed its support for the International Hockey Hall of Fame in Kingston. The first permanent building opened in Exhibition Place in 1961, and the 1993 the Hall was moved to a former Bank of Montreal building, where it remains to this day.

The Hall features over 15 exhibits covering 60,000 square feet of floor space. The usual hall of fame items are present and accounted for: memorabilia, trophies and equipment used in pivotal games or by superstars of the past fill the display cases. There are several distinct zones to the Hall.

The Esso Great Hall, located in the former bank vault, holds portraits and short biographies of every honoree. The Stanley Cup is on display here, along with the Conn Smythe Award and the Jennings Cup.

The NHL Zone is broken up into subzones of the NHL Today, NHL Retro, NHL legends, NHL Milestones and Stanley Cup Dynasties.

The NHLPA Be A Player Zone gives visitors the chance to shoot real pucks at a computer simulation of goalie Ed Belfour. They can also take the opportunity to play goalie in the Lay's Shut Out exhibit, where they can try to stop shots from players like Wayne Gretzy and Mark Messier.

The TSN/RDS Broadcast Zone shows visitors a behind-the-scenes look at what it takes to broadcast a hockey game on television and radio.

The World of Hockey Zone is a relatively new addition, and it was an effort to address complaints that the Hall was really more of an NHL Hall of Fame than a Hockey Hall of Fame. This zone displays memorabilia from international hockey's finest.

Each year in June, an 18-person committee made up of players, coaches, and others (owners, broadcasters, or referees) meet to discuss the current batch of eligible nominees. These 18 people are appointed by the NHL Board of Directors for a three-year term. There are three categories in which a person can be honored: Players, Builders, and On-Ice Officials. Builders are coaches, general managers, team owners and color commentators who have contributed to the growth of the game.

Each "class" of new honorees may include a maximum of four players, two builders and one official. No more than two of the players inducted in any given year may be female. Players must have been inactive and/or retired for three years prior to being elected to the Hall, but Builders and Officials may still be active when they are inducted. The induction ceremony takes place in Toronto every November.

FUN FACTS:

1. There is a category for media honorees, but they are not true Hall of Fame inductees. Members of the hockey media can be awarded one of two trophies in recognition of excellence: the Elmer Ferguson Memorial Award, presented by the Professional Hockey Writers' Association, and the Foster Hewitt Memorial Award, which is presented by the NHL Broadcasters' Association.
2. Alan Eagleson, who had been a long-time director of the NHLPA, was inducted into the Hall in 1989. He was later convicted of embezzling hundreds of thousands of dollars from the NHLPA Pension Fund. Dozens of other inductees petitioned the Hall for Eagleson's expulsion, and he voluntarily resigned from the Hall before he could be thrown out.
3. There have been ten players for whom the three-year rule has been waived: Dit Clapper, Maurice Richard, Ted Lindsay, Red Kelly, Terry Sawchuk, Jean Béliveau, Gordie Howe, Bobby Orr, Mario Lemieux and Wayne Gretzky.

4. Three players have come out of retirement after induction into the Hockey Hall of Fame to resume their playing careers: Gordie Howe, Guy Lafleur and Mario Lemieux.
5. As of 2016, the Hall of Fame had honored 271 players (including four women), 105 builders and 16 on-ice officials.

INTERNATIONAL HOCKEY

The NHL's Greatest Rival – The KHL

The KHL, or Kontinental Hockey League, is the successor to the Russian Superleague. It was founded in 2008 and currently boasts 29 teams in multiple countries (Belarus, China, Croatia, Finland, Kazakhstan, Latvia, Russia and Slovakia). It is considered the second-best league in the world, second only to the NHL.

The league has two conferences, East and West, and each conference has two divisions. The East conference has 15 teams, with 7 in one division and 8 in the other. The West conference has 14 teams, with 7 in each division. The league plays a total of 60 games per season, followed by playoffs. The eight top-ranked teams at the end of the regular season enter the playoffs. Its championship trophy is called the Gagarin Cup, and the top-ranked Russian team at the end of the season is awarded the title "Champion of Russia." The winner of the regular season receives the Continental Cup. Each season, the defending champions play the runner-up of the previous Gagarin Cup Finals, and the winner of that match is given the Opening Cup. In 2012, the KHL also introduced the Nadezhda Cup (Hope Cup) as a consolation tournament for the teams that did not make the Gagarin Cup playoffs. The winner of the Hope Cup gets the first overall pick in the KHL Junior Draft.

In the KHL, Russian teams may only have five foreign players on their rosters, and foreign-born goalies have limits on the number of games that they can play. Teams outside of Russia must have at least five players from their host countries.

Prior to the inaugural season, the KHL signed a number of NHL players in violation of their NHL contracts. This led to lengthy legal disputes between the two leagues. Ultimately, the International Ice Hockey Federation got involved, and the contract issues were settled by agreement between the leagues on October 4, 2010.

On September 7, 2011, the KHL was rocked by tragedy when the plane carrying the entire Lokomotiv Yaroslavl team and staff crashed immediately after take-off. There were only two survivors, both of whom died later of their injuries. To this day, September 7 is a league-wide day of mourning, and no games are scheduled on that date.

FUN FACTS:

1. During the 2004 NHL lockout, 40 NHL players went to the KHL to play.
2. The 2011 Opening Cup was awarded to Lokomotiv Yaroslavl.

3. Each year, the conference winners are awarded the very creatively named Eastern Conference Champion Cup and Western Conference Champion Cup.
4. Every year, Russian President Vladimir Putin plays in an exhibition game against KHL and former NHL players. He always scores multiple goals and his team always wins the game.
5. Players' contract interests are served by the KHL Players' Trade Union.

Hockey Beneath the Midnight Sun – Liiga, the Finnish Elite League

Founded in 1975, the SM-liiga was a successor to the SM-sarja, which was an amateur organization. Professional hockey really didn't take off in Finland until 1990, which is the first time that all players in the league were full-time athletes. In 2013, the league's name was changed simply to Liiga, or in English, the Finnish Elite League.

The league is operated by the Finnish Ice Hockey Association in an "agreement of cooperation" with league management. There are 15 teams, who play 60 matches in a quadruple round-robin season that sees every team compete against every other team in the league four times. Liiga games are 60 minutes in duration, with a five-minute 3-on-3 sudden death overtime period in the case of a tie. If the game has not been decided by the end of the overtime period, then the game goes to a shootout. In the playoffs, ties are decided by additional 20-minute overtime periods, which last until one of the teams scores.

In the post season, the top six teams automatically enter the semi-finals. Teams ranked seven through ten play a best-of-three tournament, similar to a wild card tournament, to see who gets the remaining two slots in the semi-finals. At that point, the post season series becomes best of seven. The losers of the semi-finals play for the bronze medal, while the top two teams contend for silver and gold, like in the Olympics. The champion also takes home the *Kanada-malja*, which is the league trophy. The regular season champions are awarded the *Harry Lindbladin muistopalkinto*, which is similar to the NHL's Presidents Trophy.

The season starts in mid-September and has two two-week breaks, one at the end of October so that Team Finland can play in the European Hockey Championships, and the other at Christmas. In Olympic years, the league breaks for the Games, too, so that Team Finland can compete.

The Liiga awards a number of trophies at the end of its season, which were all renamed after legendary figures in Finnish hockey in 1995. Prior to that date, all trophies were named after sponsors.

FUN FACTS:

1. The most successful team in Liiga history is TPS, also known as Turun Palloseura, which has won ten championships.
2. One of TPS's owners is former Calgary Flames goaltender Miikka Kiprusoff.
3. As of March 2008, the Liiga was ranked as the second strongest league in all of Europe.
4. The name of the league trophy, *Kanada-malja,*

translates as "Canada Bowl" in English. The trophy was donated to SM-sarja by Canada's Finnish population in 1951.
5. The Liiga has its own Hall of Fame, called the Suomen Jääkiekkomuseo.

Sweden's Pride and Joy
– The Swedish Hockey League

The Swedish Hockey League (SHL) was first founded in 1975 as Elitserien (Swedish Elite League in English, or SEL). It started out with 10 teams and eventually expanded to the current number of teams, 14. The league was re-named the SHL in 2013.

With the information just provide, you would be forgiven for believing that hockey was a recent arrival in Sweden. In actual fact, the first Swedish Ice Hockey Championship was won in 1922, only two years after American film director Raoul LeMat introduced the game to Sweden.

The SHL plays more or less in the same style as the NHL. Each game has 60 minutes of play, with two 18-minute intermissions (as opposed to 20-minute intermissions in North America). If the game is tied at the end of regulation, then the teams play a five-minute four-on-four sudden death overtime period. If the score remains unbroken, then the game goes to a shootout. In the playoffs, instead of going to the four-on-four, the teams play 20-minute sudden-death overtime periods.

The regular season in the SHL consists of 52 round-robin games followed by a best-of-seven elimination tournament involving the first through sixth seeded teams. They play every year for the LeMat Trophy.

Additional hardware handed out at the end of each season in the SEL include the Golden Puck, which is awarded to the ice hockey player of the year; the Håkan Loob Trophy for scoring leader (the only trophy in the SEL based on stats), the Guldhjälmen Trophy for league MVP, and the Årets Rookie Trophy for rookie of the year. The playoff MVP trophy was renamed the Stefan Liv Memorial Trophy in honor of Swedish goaltender Stefan Liv, who lost his life in the 2011 Lokomotiv Yaroslavl disaster.

Swedish Hockey League games are broadcast on national networks in Sweden, Finland, Denmark and Norway. During the 2004-05 NHL lockout, SHL games were also broadcast in Canada by Rogers Sportsnet.

FUN FACTS:

1. The longest SHL game in history was in 1997, in the Swedish Championship semi-finals. Leksands IF and Färjestad BK played 59 minutes of overtime (nearly three complete extra periods) before the game-winning goal was scored by Andreas Karlsson for Leksands.
2. In the 2012-13 season, the SHL was the best-attended ice hockey league in all of Europe.
3. The SHL is the second most popular professional league in Sweden, led only by the Allsvenskan

(football/soccer).
4. Djurgårdens IF has won the most titles since 1922 with a total of 16 LeMat Trophies.
5. In the modern era, the most successful team has been Färjestad BK, with nine wins since 1975.

THE COACHES

Head Coach and Union Buster – Jack Adams

John James "Jack" Adams was born on June 14, 1894 in Fort William, Ontario. He began playing hockey for the Fort William Maple Leafs of the NMHL in 1914 and went pro in 1917 with the Toronto Arenas of the NHL. He went on to play for the Vancouver Millionaires, Toronto St. Patricks and the Ottawa Senators. He won the Stanley Cup with the Senators in 1927.

In 1927, after his retirement as a player, he became head coach of the Detroit Cougars at the urging of NHL president Frank Calder. The team was not successful, and a name change in 1930 to the Detroit Falcons did nothing to break the streak of bad luck. In 1932, the team was purchased by James E. Norris and renamed the Red Wings, and he provided the funds for the team to finally hire the caliber of players they needed to move ahead. Adams served a head coach and general manager until he retired from coaching in 1947 to concentrate on his general managerial duties. Under his leadership, the Red

Wings won three Cups.

As general manager, he built up the Red Wings' farm system, which churned out players like Alex Delvecchio, Sid Abel, Terry Sawchuk, Ted Lindsay, Red Kelly and Gordie Howe. These players formed the core of the team and went on to win four Stanley Cups between 1948 and 1955. During this time, despite the success of his team, Adams showed a willingness to make blockbuster trades, earning him the nickname of "Trader Jack". He stated reason for these trades was to keep his team from becoming complacent.

In 1957, Adams traded away Ted Lindsay as revenge for Lindsay's attempts to organize the NHLPA players' union. As part of his union busting activities, he spread false rumors that Lindsay had been criticizing other players on the team, and he provided the Detroit media with a fake contract alleging that Lindsay was earning $25,000 a year, far higher than the rest of the team (and higher than his actual salary, which was $13,000). These rumors and lies helped to create a rift between Lindsay and his former linemates and also led the core of the Red Wings team to leave Detroit. He was fired as a result of his union-busting activities and falsifications in 1963.

In 1963, he became the founding president of the Central Hockey League. He died at his desk in 1966.

FUN FACTS:

1. Adams was the first coach to be suspended during the Stanley Cup Finals after an altercation with a referee about allegedly biased penalty calls. Adams punched the referee in the face in game three and was suspended for the remainder of the tournament.
2. The Jack Adams Award for coach of the year was introduced in 1974.
3. His 36-year tenure as general manager with the Red Wings is the longest in NHL history, and he served 15 of those years without a contract. He was hired with a handshake with owner James Norris.
4. He is the only man to win the Stanley Cup as a player, coach and general manager.
5. He was inducted into the Hockey Hall of Fame as a player in 1959.

"Coach Q" – Joel Quenneville

Joel Norman Quenneville was born on September 15, 1958 in Windsor, Ontario. He was drafted 21st overall by the Toronto Maple Leafs in 1978, and he played until 1991 with Toronto, Colorado Rockies, New Jersey Devils, Hartford Whalers and Washington Capitals.

He began coaching in 1996 as assistant coach with the Colorado Avalanche, when the team won the Stanley Cup. In 1997, he went on to become head coach for the St. Louis Blues. His best season with that team was in 1999-2000, when he led them to a franchise record 51 wins and their first ever President's Trophy. Unfortunately, his eighth season as head coach was an unmitigated disaster, as the Blues failed to reach the playoffs for the first time in 25 years. He was relieved of his duties in St. Louis but went to the Colorado Avalanche just in time for the 2004 season to be cancelled due the lockout. With the Avalanche, he recorded his 750th game as head coach and his 400th win.

He left the Avalanche in 2008, at which time he went to Chicago as a pro scout. One month later, he was promoted to head coach of the Blackhawks. On

December 1, 2009, he recorded his 500th win as a head coach in an 11-round shootout victory over the Columbus Blue Jackets. Finally, in 2010, he won the Stanley Cup for the first time as head coach. His 600th win came in 2011, and in 2014, he recorded his 700th win as head coach, only the third coach in NHL history to reach that milestone.

He is now the second most successful coach in NHL history, second only to Scotty Bowman, and he continues as head coach of the Blackhawks.

FUN FACTS:

1. When Chicago won the Stanley Cup in 2015, it was the first time since 1938 that the Blackhawks had won on home ice.
2. He met his wife Elizabeth while he was playing with the Hartford Whalers.
3. In 2011, he obtained US citizenship, making him a dual citizen.
4. He served as assistant coach to Team Canada in their Olympic gold medal victories in 2010 and 2014.
5. As of the 2006-07 season, he was one of only seven active coaches with 750 NHL games under his belt.

The Winningest Coach
– Scotty Bowman

Scotty Bowman holds the NHL record for most wins by a coach in league history. He has notched a staggering 1,244 regular season wins and 223 playoff victories. He has won 14 Stanley Cups, including nine as head coach, which is another NHL record. Five of his Cups came when he was in the front office staff of winning teams.

Scotty was born on September 18, 1933, in Verdun, Quebec. He played in the minors until he suffered a career-ending skull fracture. His first coaching job was with the Ottawa Junior Canadiens in the Quebec Junior Hockey League in 1956. He led the Junior Canadiens to a Memorial Cup victory in 1958.

In 1967, he became an assistant coach with the newly-formed St. Louis Blues. Halfway through that season, head coach Lynn Patrick resigned, and Scotty began his first head coaching job. Under his leadership, the Blues reached the Stanley Cup Finals in their first three years of existence. He left the Blues after the 1970-71 season due to disputes with the team's owners.

He then became head coach of the Montreal Canadiens, the defending Stanley Cup champions, after their head coach Al MacNeil was fired for favoritism toward the team's Anglophone players. Scotty, as a Quebec native, is fluent in both English and French, which led to his selection. He wanted to be named general manager of the team in addition to head coach, but the team's owners balked, so he left the Canadiens in 1979. Many of the team's core players left when Scotty did, and this effectively ended Montreal's dynasty.

He went on to be the head coach and general manager for the Buffalo Sabres, where he served as general manager until 1987, when he was fired because the team missed the playoffs. He moved on to become an analyst for the CBC's *Hockey Night in Canada*.

In 1990, he became the Director of Player Personnel for the Pittsburgh Penguins. He was elected to the Hockey Hall of Fame as a builder in 1991. That same year, he became head coach of the Penguins, and in the 1992-93 season, Pittsburgh set an NHL record for most consecutive wins (17). They also set a franchise record that season of 119 overall points. He left the Penguins due to a contract dispute.

He wasn't unemployed for long. Scotty became the head coach of the Detroit Red Wings in 1993, and the team won the Western Conference championship his first year. The next year, the team made it to the Stanley Cup finals, but they were swept by San Jose. The 1995-96 season saw the Wings make it to the Western Conference Finals, where they lost to the

Colorado Avalanche. Things finally came together for them in 1997, when the Red Wings swept Philadelphia in the Cup Finals. They repeated the feat in 1998, when they swept the Washington Capitals for the Stanley Cup.

Scotty announced his retirement a head coach in February 2002, and that year the Red Wings won the Cup again, dedicating the win to him and to injured player Vladimir Konstantinov. Scotty donned an old pair of skates so that he could take a victory lap with the Cup.

He stayed on with the Red Wings in the front office until 2008, when he became the Senior Advisor of Hockey Operations for the Chicago Blackhawks.

FUN FACTS:

1. His son, Stan Bowman, is the general manager of the Chicago Blackhawks.
2. In 2003, he was given a star on Canada's Walk of Fame.
3. He was made an Officer of the Order of Canada in 2012.
4. Rumor has it that when he was head coach of the Red Wings, he frequently got lost in the labyrinthine bowels of Joe Louis Arena and needed to be rescued.
5. He coached Team Canada in the Canada Cup in 1976 (gold) and 1981 (silver).

THE PLAYERS

The Great 8 – Alexander Ovechkin

Alexander Mikhailovich Ovechkin was born on September 17, 1985 in Moscow, Russia. His father, Mikhail, was a professional soccer player. His mother, Tatyana, won Olympic gold with the Soviet Union's women's basketball team in 1976 and 1980. He became enamored of hockey at the age of two and enrolled in hockey school at the age of 8. His older brother, Sergei, who introduced him to the game, died in a car accident when Alex was 10 years old. He has dedicated his career to Sergei's memory.

He began playing for Dynamo Moscow in the Russian Superleague when he was 16 years old. In 2004, he was drafted first overall in the NHL Entry Draft by the Washington Capitals. He played in Russia during the NHL lockout, but for the 2005-06 season, he signed with the Capitals for the rookie maximum of $984,200 per season on a three-year contract. Additional bonuses built into his contract brought his salary closer to $3.9 million a year. This was the richest rookie contract in NHL history.

He scored two goals in his very first NHL game, which was a hint of things to come. On January 13, 2006, he scored his first NHL hat trick, and on January 16, 2016, he scored what has come to be known only as "The Goal". He was tripped while driving toward the net, but while falling and with only one hand on his stick, he managed to get the puck into the net. That goal is still a favorite on YouTube. On February 1, 2006, he was named NHL Rookie of the Month and Offensive Player of the Month, only the third played in history to win both honors simultaneously. He finished the 2005-06 season leading all NHL rookies in goals, points, power play goals and shots. He was third overall in the NHL scoring race. His 425 shots led the league that year, and it set the NHL rookie record. It was also the fourth highest in NHL history. He was named to the NHL First All-Star Team, the first rookie to be honored that way in 15 years, and he won the Calder Cup as rookie of the year.

In the 2007-08 season, he signed a 13-year contract extension work $124 million, or $9.5 million per year. This is the richest contract in NHL history. Remarkably, he negotiated the contract himself without the assistance of an agent. He still represents himself in this way.

His second pro season was his second 50-goal season. In fact, he scored 60 goals, the first player to do so since the 1995-96 season. He was the first NHL player to score at least 40 even-strength goals in one season since Pavel Bure in 1999. At season's end, he walked away from the NHL Awards with the Rocket Richard Award, the Art Ross Trophy, the Hart Trophy and the Lester B. Pearson Award (now called the Ted Lindsay Award). He was the first player in NHL history to win all four major awards in one season.

In 2008-09, he scored his 250th goal, making him only the fourth player in league history to reach that mark in four seasons. He scored his first playoff hat trick and won the Rocket Richard, Hart and Lester B. Pearson Awards once again. He was the third player in Washington Capitals franchise history to score three consecutive 50-goal seasons.

The 2009-10 season saw things get a little tougher. Ovechkin, or "Ovi," as he is known, had always been known as much for his hitting as for his scoring. This season, he got carried away and was suspended twice for brutal hits on opposing players. Despite this inglorious accomplishment, he was named team captain on January 5, 2010, making him both the first European captain and the second youngest in team history. He scored his 500th point on February 5, 2010, only the fifth player in NHL history to score 500 points in five seasons. He won the Ted Lindsay Award (formerly the Lester B. Pearson Award), making him only the second player in league history to win the award three consecutive times. He was also the first play in NHL history to be voted a First Team All-Star in each of his first five seasons.

In the 2010-11 season, he scored his 600th career point and 300th career goal, and he also notched his first NHL fighting major. The following season, with a coaching change at the Capitals and a third suspension for an illegal hit, Ovi's numbers began to slide. He was being ordered to play a defensive game, something that is anathema to a sniper like him, and his numbers showed his struggle with the change.

In 2013-14, there was another coaching change, and Ovi was allowed to be Ovi again. He returned to form and scored his 400th career goal. He won his third Rocket Richard and Hart Trophies that season. The next season, he became the sixth player in NHL history to have six 50-goal seasons. The 2015-16 season saw him rack up his 500th goal. He became only the third player in the league to ever have seven or more 50-goal seasons. In the 2016-17 season (which was still being played as of this writing), he scored his 1000th point, tying Rocket Richard's record on Montreal ice.

FUN FACTS:

1. Asteroid 257261 Ovechkin was named in his honor by astrophysicist Leonid Elenin.
2. He holds the NHL record for most seasons with 10 or more game-winning goals.
3. He once had a feud with fellow Russian Yevgeni Malkin, which allegedly began when Ovechkin punched Malkin's agent in a Moscow nightclub in the offseason. The rift was allegedly mended through mediation by Russian star Ilya Kovalchuk.
4. He scored the fastest overtime goal in NHL

history, lighting the lamp just six seconds into play.
5. He has won the Kharlamov Trophy, awarded to the best Russian-born player in the NHL, in 2006, 2007, 2008, 2009, 2010, 2014 and 2015.

Fabulous Number
Four - Bobby Orr

Bobby Orr is considered one of the greatest players of all time. He was born in Canada in 1948 and began playing at the age of five. He worked his way up through the junior hockey ranks, but already showed his immense promise when he joined the Oshawa Generals at 14, when he was an Ontario Hockey League (OHL) all-star for three consecutive years. The Generals where the farm team for the NHL's Boston Bruins, and he joined the Bruins in 1966. Prior to his arrival, the Bruins had not made the playoffs since 1959, and hadn't won the Stanley Cup since 1941. With Bobby on the team, they won the Cup twice. Bobby himself was the playoff MVP in both 1970 and 1972, scoring the title-winning goal in each championship.

Bobby's first professional contract was negotiated by an agent, making him one of the first hockey players in the league's history to have be represented in contract talks. He was the highest-paid rookie ever in the league, and his was the first million-dollar contract in the NHL. He played with the Bruins from 1966 to 1975, when he moved via free agency to the

Chicago Blackhawks.

He represented his homeland in international competition, as well. He had suffered serious knee injuries during his playing career, which had forced him to sit out the 1971 Summit Series, which saw Russia and Canada go head to head. He finally got the chance to lace them up for Canada in the 1976 World Cup, when he was named MVP despite the serious pain he was in from his knee. One of his teammates, Darryl Sittler, commented that on one leg, Bobby was better than anybody else was on two.

Unfortunately, Bobby's knee injuries would bring his career to a premature end. Although he signed with the Blackhawks, he only played 26 games in three seasons as his knee kept him on the bench most of the time. He retired in 1978 at the age of thirty. When he retired, he held the NHL record for most goals, most points, and most assists by a defenseman. He was so extraordinary that he was ranked 10th in those measures overall.

The Hockey Hall of Fame has a three-year rule, stating that players must be retired for that long before they can be inducted into the Hall. For Bobby, they made an exception. He was inducted into the Hall of Fame the very next year, at the age of 31. He was the youngest player to ever be enshrined in the Hall of Fame.

The Boston Bruins retired his number, number 4, in 1979. Boston fans in attendance for the event cheered so loudly and so long that Bobby was never able to give his acceptance speech, and the remainder of the program had to be cancelled.

After his playing days were over, Bobby stayed in hockey, this time as a players' agent. He was also instrumental in lawsuits against corrupt agents and the Hockey Hall of Fame itself, establishing the rights of hockey players to the income they earned while they were on the ice. He is still working as an agent today.

FUN FACTS:

1. Bobby Orr was awarded the Order of Canada, which was bestowed upon him by Queen Elizabeth II.
2. The Order of Canada was not his only award from the sovereign. He was also given the Queen Elizabeth II Diamond Jubilee Medal in 2012, honoring his significant accomplishments as a Canadian.
3. "The Goal" – one of the most famous hockey photographs ever taken shows Bobby Orr flying through the air, perpendicular to the ground. The photograph was taken by Ray Lussier just after Bobby had scored the championship-winning goal in the 1970 Stanley Cup finals. He was flying because he had just been tripped by a defenseman for the opposing team.
4. In 1970, he won the Norris Trophy, the Art Ross Trophy, the Hart Trophy and the Conn Smythe Trophy – the only player in history to win four of the NHL's top awards in one season.
5. Bobby's son, Darren, works with him at Orr

Hockey Group, representing players as an agent.
6. Bobby has been a frequent contributor of time and money to various charities. The Multiple Sclerosis Society awarded him the Multiple Sclerosis Silver Hope Chest in 1980 recognizing his charitable work.

The Greek God - Chris Chelios

Christos Kostas "Chris" Chelios, a/k/a Cheli, was born in on January 5, 1962, in Evergreen Park, Illinois. He moved with his parents to southern California when he was in high school, and although he had enjoyed stand-out youth hockey career, he was unable to continue playing in SoCal and as a result was never recruited by any colleges in the United States. He nonetheless received a scholarship from the United States International University, which was located in San Diego, California, and was the only NCAA Division I hockey team west of the Rocky Mountains at that time.

He found to his dismay that he was surrounded by players who were bigger, stronger, and more experienced at the junior hockey level, and he failed to make the team. He tried his luck in Canada and ended up needing to borrow money to return home. He considered quitting hockey all together, but he ended up growing three inches and gaining almost 40 pounds in muscle, overcoming some of the size deficit he had experienced.

In 1981, he was drafted by the Montreal Canadiens as a defenseman and moved to the University of

Wisconsin-Madison, where he played two years for the Wisconsin Badgers. He was one of the top college-level players in the United States at that time, and was selected for Team USA for the 1981-82 World Junior Championships. He played in the NCAA Men's Ice Hockey Championship with Wisconsin in 1983 and was selected to the all-tournament team as well as to the second WCHA (Western Collegiate Hockey Association) all-star team. He joined Team USA at the 1984 Olympics at Sarajevo and again at the 1984 Canada Cup.

He played with the Montreal Canadiens from 1984 to 1990, where he became known for the offensive side of his play. He scored 64 points in 74 games and was selected for the 1985 NHL All-Rookie Team. He was also a nominee for the Calder Cup (losing to Mario Lemieux). In the 1985-86 season, he won his first Stanley Cup.

Chelios had a breakout season in 1988-89. He played 80 games and scored 73 points, with an overall +35. He was named to the NHL All-Star First Team and won the James Norris Memorial Trophy as defenseman of the year. He became notorious during that year's Eastern Conference Finals for an allegedly dirty hit on Brian Propp of the Philadelphia Flyers, which left Propp with a serious concussion. On the last game of the series, Philadelphia goalie Ron Hextall retaliated by attacking Chelios, and Hextall earned himself a 12-game suspension.

In 1989-90, Chelios was co-captain of the Canadiens. On June 29, 1990, after an off-ice incident where he got into a fight with two police officers after urinating outside a bar in Madison, Wisconsin, he was traded to the Chicago Blackhawks.

He stayed with the Blackhawks until 1999, and he continued to score at a rapid pace. He got 64 points in his first season in Chicago, making his way to the Second NHL All-Star Team. The Blackhawks made it to the Stanley Cup Finals in 1992, but were swept by Pittsburgh. IN 1992-93, he scored another 73 points and took home his second Norris Trophy.

When the NHL lockout came in 1994-95, Chelios went to play in the Swiss National League A for the team EHC Biel.

He returned to Chicago in 1995-96, and that season he again led all defensemen in scoring with 72 points and won his third Norris Trophy. He became captain of the Blackhawks in 1995, and that summer, he joined Team USA in their highest international win at that time, defeating Canada in the 1996 World Cup of Hockey.

Chelios was traded to the Detroit Red Wings in 1999 and stayed with that team until 2009, helping to win the Stanley Cup in 2002 and 2008. In 2005, when Red Wings Captain Steve Yzerman retired, he became the active leader for most games played. On April 21, 2007, he became the oldest defenseman to ever score a short-handed playoff goal.

In 2006, Chelios went to the Olympic Games in Turin, Italy as the captain of Team USA. He became the first player to take part in two Olympic hockey tournaments, 22 years after his first.

He re-signed with the Red Wings for the 2007-08

campaign and became the second oldest player in the history of the NHL. He was 45. (Only Gordie Howe, who was playing in the NHL at 52, was older.) He played his 248th playoff game in April 2008, breaking the record previously held by goalie Patrick Roy. That June, he became the oldest active player to win the Stanley Cup.

He signed another contract with the Wings, but he was "send down" to the team's AHL affiliate, the Grand Rapids Griffins, where he became the oldest player in that lower league's history. At the end of the 2008-09 season, he was a finalist for the Bill Masterton Memorial Trophy.

Chelios officially retired on August 31, 2010 at 48 years of age. That same day, he was named as Advisor to Hockey Operations, reporting to general manager Ken Holland.

In 2016, Chelios began a coaching career, being named assistant coach to Team USA in the 2016 World Junior Ice Hockey Championships. He went on to be an assistant coach to the Detroit Red Wings in the 2016-17 season.

FUN FACTS:

1. Chelios owns and operates two restaurants/sports bars in the Detroit Area, called Cheli's Chili. His chili was also marketed in the frozen section of local grocery stores.
2. He trained and surfing champion Laird Hamilton trained with the 2004 US bobsled team in a failed attempt to create a Greek bobsled team for the

2006 Winter Olympics.
3. He has a home in Malibu, California, which is the center for the so-called "Malibu Mob": Chelios, actors John McGinley, John Cusack, Kelsey Grammer, and Tony Danza; surfer Laird Hamilton; beach volleyball pro Gabrielle Reece; tennis player John McEnroe; and musicians Tim Commerford and Kid Rock.
4. Chelios's sons Dean and Jake both played for the Michigan State Spartans hockey teams, playing for two years on the same team. They are both now in the minor pros.
5. He appeared in the movie *The Cutting Edge* with actor D. B. Sweeney. Chelios is the godfather of Sweeney's son, Cade.

"Mr. Hockey" - Gordie Howe

Gordie Howe was known as "Mr. Hockey" because of his longevity and raw talent. He still holds the record for the most games and most seasons played. He began his professional career in 1946 and did not retire until 1980, playing an amazing twenty-six seasons. He was in the top ten in the NHL for scoring for twenty-one consecutive years. He also played in the World Hockey Association (WHA) for seven years. He is the only player to have played professionally in six decades.

He was born in Canada and began his NHL career with the Detroit Red Wings. Gordie was a physical presence on the ice with a penchant for fighting, but he was also a consummate goal scorer. He scored his first NHL goal in his very first game when he was only 18 years old (the NHL rule barring players younger than 20 was still several years in the future). He led the Red Wings to four Stanley Cups. He played on a line with Sid Abel and Ted Lindsay, and they became known as "the Production Line" because of their scoring ability. The nickname was also a tip of the hat to the automotive industry in Detroit. In the 1949-1950 season, the Production

Line finished as the top three goal scorers in the league.

Gordie won a number of awards, including six Hart Memorial Trophies as league MVP. The only player to ever win more Hart trophies is Wayne Gretzky. In fact, most of Gordie's records for scoring stood until Gretzky came along. Gretzky named Gordie Howe as his childhood idol, and the two men became good friends. Gretzky served as a pall bearer at Gordie's funeral in 2016.

In 1972, he joined the Houston Aeros, where he played alongside his sons Mark and Marty. All three Howes moved on to play for the Hartford Whalers. He won the WHA league MVP award in 1974 at the age of 46.

FUN FACTS:

1. The Gordie Howe Hat Trick is scored when a player gets one goal, one assist, and one fight in a single game. In his entire career, Gordie Howe himself only accomplished this feat twice.
2. A bridge connecting the United States and Canada, still under construction, has been named the Gordie Howe International Bridge. The bridge connects the cities of Detroit, Michigan and Windsor, Ontario.
3. He was inducted into the Hockey Hall of Fame in 1972, and the Detroit Red Wings retired his number, number 9, that same year.
4. He played 2,421 games with the NHL, a feat that has never been surpassed.

5. He has received numerous awards from the sovereign of Canada, including the Order of Canada, the Queen Elizabeth II Silver Jubilee Award, the Queen Elizabeth II Golden Jubilee Award, and the Queen Elizabeth II Diamond Jubilee Award.

The Ageless Wonder - Jaromir Jagr

Jaromir Jagr is arguably the best Czech hockey player to ever lace up skates. He was born on February 15, 1972, in Kladno, Czechoslovakia (now the Czech Republic). He began skating at the age of three, and by the time he was 15, he was competing at the highest level in his homeland. He played for the Czech professional team HC Kladno, and at 17, he became the youngest member of the Czech national team. He was the first Czech player to be drafted by the NHL when he was selected fifth overall by the Pittsburgh Penguins in the 1990 NHL Entry Draft.

He was a member of the Penguins team that won back-to-back Stanley Cups in 1991 and 1992, and he was the youngest player to ever score a goal in the Stanley Cup Finals (20 years old). He played with the Penguins from 1990 to 2001, and during that time he won the Art Ross Trophy, the Hart Memorial Trophy, and the Lester B. Pearson Award. He became the second player in Penguins history to score 1,000 points.

He moved to the Washington Capitals in 2001, signing what was at the time the largest contract in

NHL history, $77 million over seven years with an option for an eighth year. He had lost his scoring touch, however, and despite his presence on the team and the high expectations that the team's management had for him, he failed to reach the playoffs or the NHL All-Star Team for the first time in his career.

Jagr was traded to the New York Rangers in 2004. As a result of the new collective bargaining agreement between the NHL and the NHLPA, his salary was reduced to $7.8 million, the league maximum. He returned to his homeland to play for HC Kladno and later went to Russia to play for Avangard Omsk in the Russian Superleague during the 2004 lockout.

At the beginning of the 2005-2006 season, most pundits picked the Rangers as the worst team in the league. Jagr announced, however, that the team would reach the playoffs. He began the season with a return to his prior form, scoring ten or more goals in the first ten games of the season, only the fourth player in NHL history to do so. In 2006, he scored his 1,400th point, scored more than 100 points in the season, and won his third Lester B. Pearson Award.

In the 2006-07 season, he scored his 600th career goal and his 1,500th career point. He is the 12th NHL player to score that many points, and he is the fourth fastest to do so. He scored his 30th goal of the season, making the 2006-07 season his 15th consecutive campaign with 30 or more goals, tying the NHL record.

In 2008, Jagr became an unrestricted free agent, and the Rangers declined to enter into contract negotiations with him. He opted to go to Russia, where he played for two years for Avangard Omsk of the KHL. He was named captain of Avangard in January 2009.

In 2011, Jagr returned to the NHL, signing with the Philadelphia Flyers. He scored his 1,600th career point in his first game with the Flyers, setting the tune for season among the top scorers in the league.

He moved on to the Dallas Stars in 2012, but because of the NHL lockout, he returned to his homeland to pay for Rytiri Kladno. He played his first game for Dallas in January 2013, after the lockout was over. He scored his 1,000th assist, only the 12th player in NHL history and the first non-Canadian to do so. Despite this, he was traded in April to Boston, and he tied the NHL record for the most game-winning goals (118) with his new team. When the Bruins went to the 2013 Stanley Cup Finals, he set the record for the longest gap between Finals appearances - 21 years.

In 2013, Jagr signed a one-year deal with the New Jersey Devils. He scored his first goal with the Devils on the 23rd anniversary of his first NHL goal. In November 2013, tied Mario Lemieux for ninth place in all-time scoring leaders. He continued to score, ending the season with 1,755 points, tying Steve Yzerman for sixth place on the all-time scoring list. He also scored his 700th career NHL goal.

He played for the Devils in the 2014-15 season,

during which he became the oldest player in NHL history to score a hat trick, and added to his gaudy all-time scoring number for a total of 1,772, moving into fifth place in league history. Despite these superlatives, he was again traded, this time to the Florida Panthers. Before the season was over, he would reach the 2,000 point mark and his 800th NHL goal, moving into fourth place on the NHL all-time scoring list. In that year's postseason, he became the fifth NHL player to ever score 200 points in the playoffs.

He continues to play for the Florida Panthers, and on October 20, 2016, he became only the third player in NHL history to score 750 goals.

FUN FACTS:

1. He was the first player to score a goal in 53 different NHL arenas.
2. While he was captain of Avangard, he had a teammate literally die on him. Alexei Cherepanov collapsed onto Jagr while they were sitting together on the bench during the game. He died due to untreated myocarditis. Cherepanov was only 19 years old.
3. He and the Czech National Team won a gold medal at the 1998 Nagano Olympic Games.
4. He holds the record as the oldest NHL player to score 60 points in a season.
5. He has been selected for the NHL All-Star Team a whopping 13 times.

Super Mario - Mario Lemieux

Joseph Roger Mario Lemieux was born on October 5, 1965, in Montreal, Quebec, Canada. He began playing hockey at the age of three in his parents' basement, using improvised equipment (wooden spoons for skates, bottle caps as pucks). He began organized play with the Laval Voisins of the Quebec Major Junior Hockey League (QMJHL), and he went on to break many QMJHL records, including the number of points in a season (282 points in 70 games). He finished his time in that league with 562 points in three seasons. He was drafted by the Pittsburgh Penguins in 1984, and despite the team's financial woes at that time, he was signed to a two-year contract worth $600,000 plus a signing bonus of $150,000.

In his very first NHL game, on his first shift, he stole the puck from Ray Bourque and scored his first NHL goal. Bourque was no slouch - he would in fact go on to be inducted into the Hall of Fame. In his first season, Lemieux went to the NHL All-Star Game and was the first rookie to be named as the All-Star Game's MVP. He scored 100 points his first season and picked up the Calder Trophy for rookie of the year.

In the 1985-86 season, he finished second in scoring for the league with 141 points, coming in behind Wayne Gretzky's record-breaking 215 points. He won the Lester B. Pearson Award as the best regular-season player as voted by his peers. The following season, he missed 17 games due to a back injury, but his point production slipped, causing the Penguins to miss the playoffs. That summer, though, he went to the Canada Cup and set a tournament record of 11 goals in 9 games.

The 1987-88 season saw him win his seventh consecutive Art Ross Trophy as the league's points leader. He also won his first Hart Trophy and was named the All-Star Game MVP. The Pittsburgh Penguins finished one point out of the playoffs, but they finally had their first winning season since 1979.

In the 1988-89 season, Lemieux led the league in assists (tied with Gretzky) and had 85 goals for a total of 199 points. The only other player in NHL history to score more goals was Gretzky. He set several NHL records that season (second player to score over 70 goals in two seasons, fourth player to ever score 50 goals in 50 games, and the only player to score 13 shorthanded goals in one season) and finally led the Penguins back to the playoffs. On December 31, 1988, he did the nearly unthinkable and scored eight points in a single game against the New Jersey Devils, becoming the only player in NHL history to score every kind of point possible in the same game: power play, penalty shot, even-strength, shorthanded and empty net. He tied the NHL for scoring in a single playoff games (both points and goals), most goals in a single playoff period, and most assists in a postseason period.

In the 1989-90 season, Lemieux's back injury worsened. He had a herniated disc which developed an infection, and he required surgical intervention in the off season. In 1990-91, he missed 50 games, but returned to the lineup to play, even though he was in a great deal of pain. He won the Conn Smythe as the playoffs' most valuable player.

The 1991-92 season saw Lemieux struggling with injuries, but even so, he won his third Art Ross Trophy and helped the Penguins sweep the Chicago Blackhawks in the Stanley Cup Finals. He earned his second consecutive Conn Smythe Trophy and scored 78 points in the combined 1991 and 1992 playoffs, which was the second-best two-year playoff scoring tally in NHL history.

He started the 1992-93 season playing well, but in January 1993, he was diagnosed with Hodgkin's lymphoma. He sat out two months' worth of games while he received aggressive radiation treatment. On the day of his last radiation treatment, he returned to the ice in Philadelphia, where the Flyers' home crowd gave him a rare standing ovation. His return helped Pittsburgh go on a 1993 NHL-record 17 consecutive wins to finish as the top in the league for the first time in team history. In the games after his recovery from cancer, he scored an amazing 2.67 points per game, earning his second straight scoring title, which was also his fourth overall. He also won the Pearson Trophy for the second time and his first Bill Masterton Memorial Trophy.

In July 1993, he underwent more surgery on his back, and he missed the first ten games of the season. Over the course of the season, his back trouble caused him to miss a total of 48 additional games. He took a leave of absence in 1994 due to the fatigue caused by his cancer treatment, but he returned for another great season in 1995-96, when he scored his 500th career goal during his 650th career NHL game.

The 1996-97 season would prove to be his last due to injury and illness, but he finished out in grand style, scoring his 600th career goal and notching another 100-point season, his tenth such milestone. He announced in April 1997 that he would be retiring after the playoffs. The Penguins were eliminated by Philadelphia in the first round, but in his very last game, he scored a goal and an assist, and he received another standing ovation on Flyers ice.

The three-year waiting period was waived for him, and he was inducted into the Hockey Hall of Fame in November 1997.

The Penguins declared bankruptcy in 1998, and Lemieux made a bid to change his salary to equity, giving him controlling interest and therefore partial ownership in the club. The bankruptcy court approved his bid, and Lemieux undertook to pay every debt that the club owed. He achieved that goal in August 2005 when the last bill was paid. He was the first NHL player to become a majority owner of his former team.

In late 2000, he staged a comeback, returning to the ice on behalf of Pittsburgh against the Toronto Maple

Leafs. He scored an assist in his first 33 seconds of play, and ended the game with three points. He finished the 2000-01 season with the highest points-per-game average of any player in the NHL.

He continued to play at a high level until 2005, when he retired again. This time, it was permanent - he had been diagnosed with atrial fibrillation. He has continued as part-owner of the Penguins to this day.

FUN FACTS:

1. The same year he was diagnosed with Hodgkin's lymphoma, he founded the Mario Lemieux Foundation to fund medical research projects.
2. He was successful on the international stage, as well, winning gold in the 2002 Olympic Games and the 2004 World Cup, in addition to the 1987 Canada Cup.
3. He has opened his home to new players on his time, including Sidney Crosby, who lived with Lemieux and his family for many years before finally buying a home of his own.
4. Quebec Premier Jean Charest granted him the title of Knight in 2009.
5. He was given a space on Canada's Walk of Fame in 2004.

The Devils' Own - Martin Brodeur

Martin Brodeur was born on May 6, 1972 in Montreal, Canada. His father, Denis, was a bronze medal winner with Team Canada in the 1956 Olympics and the official photographer for the Montreal Canadiens. Although Brodeur started his hockey career as a forward, he switched to playing as a goaltender in youth hockey and never looked back.

He was drafted by the New Jersey Devils in the first round of the 1990 NHL Entry Draft and began to play in the NHL in 1991. He won his debut game and played in one playoff game. He spent the next few seasons in the AHL, but he was called up to the NHL permanently in the 1993-94 season. He won the Calder Trophy and finished the season in second place in GAA (goals-against average) and fourth in save percentage. It was an auspicious debut for what would prove to be a stellar career.

In his second NHL season, 1994-95, Brodeur backstopped the New Jersey Devils all the way to the Stanley Cup. He held the Detroit Red Wings to only seven goals in four games.

In 1995, he was named a starter in the All-Star game

and stopped every shot that he faced. He finished fourth in voting for the Vezina Trophy and played with Team Canada in the World Cup, winning a silver medal.

In 1997, Brodeur scored a playoff goal by shooting the puck the length of the ice and into an open net. He was the second goalie in NHL history to score in the playoffs, and only the fifth overall. In that same season, he finished with the lowest GAA in 30 years and won the Jennings Trophy. He had also notched 10 shutouts during the regular season.

In the 1998-99 season, Brodeur again was nominated for the Vezina Trophy and started in his fourth All-Star Game.

During the 1999-2000 season, he scored his second goal. He won 43 games that season and led the Devils to another Stanley Cup.

He won more than 40 games in the 2000-01 season for the third time in his career, and made his sixth All-Star Game appearance. The Devils went to the Stanley Cup Finals, and although they were defeated in seven games, Brodeur recorded four shutouts during the playoffs.

In 2002-03, he won his first Vezina Trophy and also took home another Jennings. He was nominated for the Hart Trophy and was once again a starter at the All-Star Game. The Devils won the Stanley Cup again with a total of seven playoff shutouts, an NHL record.

During the 2003-04 season, he again won the Vezina and Jennings trophies, and he was once again a finalist for the Hart Trophy and an All-Star Game starter.

After the 2004-05 season was cancelled due to the lockout, the league instituted a rule limiting the area of ice where a goalie was permitted to handle the puck. Because Brodeur was a known puck handler, this became known as the "Brodeur Rule."

In the 2005-06 season, he set NHL records with five consecutive 40-win seasons and ten consecutive 30-win seasons. He won the Vezina for the third year in a row. The following season, 2006-07, saw him setting or tying more NHL records, including most wins in a single season and all-time wins in the playoffs. In November 2007, he became the second goalie in NHL history to win 500 games.

He began setting records hand over fist in 2009. He set the NHL record for most wins by a goalie, most minutes played, and most regular-season shutouts. In 2009-10, he led the league in wins, shutouts, games played and minutes played and won his fifth Jennings Trophy.

During the 2011-12 playoffs, he recorded his 100th playoff victory, only the second goalie in NHL history to reach that milestone. He set the NHL record for career playoff shutouts (24). The following season, he scored his third goal, this time on the power play.

In 2014, he left the Devils and signed a tryout contract with the St. Louis Blues, but injuries were starting to cost him, and he retired in 2015.

FUN FACTS:

1. He has won two Olympic gold medals (2002 and 2010).
2. His son Anthony was drafted by the New Jersey Devils in the 2013 NHL Entry Draft, and Martin was asked to announce the selection.
3. He is co-owner of Montreal restaurant La Pizzeria Etc. with former teammate Sheldon Souray.
4. Brodeur holds NHL records in all-time number of regular season wins, losses, shutouts and games played.
5. He is the only goalie in NHL history to record eight 40-win seasons.

The Rocket - Maurice Richard

Joseph Henri Maurice Richard was born on August 4, 1921, in Montreal. He started skating at the age of four, but did not start to play organized hockey until he was 14 years old. He was an outstanding scorer in the Quebec Senior Hockey League, but in 1941 he crashed into the boards and broke his ankle. The injury was sufficiently bad that he was deemed unfit for combat when he tried to enlist in the Canadian armed forces to fight in World War Two.

He joined the Montreal Canadiens during the 1942-43 season, but his rookie season was cut short by a broken leg. He made a second attempt to join the military, but he was again rejected. His left ankle was permanently deformed from his earlier break, which had failed to heal properly. The injury forced him to alter his skating style.

He returned to the Canadiens in 1943-44, and he played in 46 of the team's 50 games. He led the team in goals, and the Canadiens won the Cup. He led the league in playoff goals that year.

In the 1944-45 season, he broke the NHL records for most points in one game and in most goals in a season. He became the first player to ever score 50 goals in 50 games. His next few seasons were spotty due to injury, but in 1949-50, he posted 43 goals on the season and led the league in goals scored for the third time. In 1950-51, he scored his 271st career goal, which made him Montreal's all-time highest goal scorer.

He became the first NHL player ever to score at least 20 goals in ten full season when he scored his 325th goal in the 1952-53 season. The Canadiens once again won the Stanley Cup that year. In 1953-54, he was the league scoring leader, and he scored his 400th career goal.

Richard was known for his temper, something that had attracted unwelcome attention from NHL president Clarence Campbell. After an on-ice altercation in Boston that nearly saw him arrested, he was suspended by Campbell for the remainder of the season, including the playoffs. In Quebec, the suspension was seen as an assault on the French-speaking population by the English-speaking establishment. On March 17, 1955, a fan threw a tear bomb in the Montreal Forum, causing the evacuation of the arena. The fleeing fans encountered demonstrators outside, and the resulting conflict involving nearly 20,000 people became known as the Richard Riot.

In 1955-56, Richard returned to the ice and led the Canadiens to another Stanley Cup championship. In 1956-57, he was named team captain, and under his leadership, Montreal won the Cup five consecutive seasons. Richard himself won a total of nine Cups.

In 1958-59, he was the oldest player in the NHL, and he retired the next year, saying that the game was now too fast for him.

FUN FACTS:

1. The Hockey Hall of Fame waived its waiting period for Richard, inducting him into the Hall in 1961.
2. He was the league's all-time scoring leader in goals when he retired.
3. Richard was appointed to the Queen's Privy Council for Canada in 1992.
4. The Maurice "Rocket" Richard Trophy was created in 1999, and it is awarded every year to the NHL's leading goal scorer.
5. When Richard died in 2000, he was given a state funeral by the province of Quebec. He was the first non-politician to receive this honor, and his lying in state was attended by 115,000 people.

"Sid the Kid" – Sidney Crosby

Sidney Patrick Crosby was born on August 7, 1987, in Halifax, Nova Scotia, Canada. He learned to skate at age 3 and had already started to attract media attention in the minors. He gave his first press interview when he was only seven years old. During his stellar minor and junior hockey career, he was often the points leader on his teams, as well as in his leagues. People were expecting great things.

He was drafted first overall in the 2005 NHL Entry Draft, selected by the Pittsburgh Penguins. His first NHL game was played on October 5, 2005, when he got an assist on the first goal of the season. His first NHL goal came only three days later. To the surprise (and some dismay) of Penguins fans and hockey intelligentsia, head coach Michel Therrien named Sidney the assistant team captain on December 18, 2005. He was only 18 years old, and many people thought he lacked the experience and maturity for such responsibility.

In his first season, he set a franchise record for number of assistant and points by a rookie. He was the youngest player in NHL history to score 100 points in one season, and the first rookie to earn 100 penalty minutes and 100 points in one season. Unfortunately for Sidney, his propensity for complaining to the referees about his penalties earned him a reputation for being a whiner, something he has yet to shake.

In the 2006-07 season, he scored his first career hat trick, and he finished as the league scoring leader at 19 years old. He was the youngest player to win the Art Ross Trophy and the youngest scoring champion in any North American professional sport. On May 31, 2007, he was named team captain, the youngest in NHL history. At the end of the season, he also won the Hart Trophy and the Lester B. Pearson Award (now called the Ted Lindsay Award). He was the youngest player in NHL history to win the Pearson and the second youngest to win the Hart, right behind Wayne Gretzky. He was also the youngest player to be named to the NHL First All-Star Team.

During the 2007-08 season, he signed a five-year contract extension with Pittsburgh. He went on to score his first Gordie Howe hat trick (a goal, an assist and a fight in the same game), and he also led his team to the Stanley Cup Finals.

His 2008-09 season came with more superlatives. He scored 100 goals, 300 points and 200 assists on his way to winning the Stanley Cup. He was youngest team captain to take the Cup since 1895. He followed up his championship season with a 2009-10 campaign that saw him take home the Rocket Richard Trophy and the Mark Messier Award for leadership.

The 2010-11 season started out well, with Sidney

going on a 25-game point streak. Then, on January 1, 2011, while playing in the Winter Classic against Alex Ovechkin's Washington Capitals, he sustained a concussion as a result of a hard hit. He was hit again just five days later, and the resulting concussion syndrome caused him to miss the rest of the season. Although he played only 41 of the season's 80 games, he was still led all other Pittsburgh players in points, an NHL record for the fewest games by a team scoring leader.

His concussion woes continued in the 2011-12 season, and he missed the first 20 games due to his injury. He returned to play in November, but concussion symptoms returned in December, and he stopped playing again until March 2012. Nevertheless, he still scored his 600th point. He also got into a bit of controversy over a bit of bad sportsmanship involving the Philadelphia Flyers' Jakub Voracek and a wayward glove (Voracek dropped his glove and was reaching to pick it up when Crosby hit it with his stick to send it farther away from its owner). Crosby was unrepentant in his after-game press conference.

During the 2012-13 lockout, Sidney often attended the meetings between the NHL and the NHLPA. When play resumed, he was back to his old form until March 30, 2013, when he was hit in the mouth by teammate Brooks Orpik's slapshot. He suffered a fractured jaw and required several rounds of reconstructive dental surgery. At the end of the season, he won the Ted Lindsay Award.

The 2013-14 season saw him play 80 games for the

first time since the 2009-10 season, and he led the league in assists and points. He won his second Art Ross Trophy and his third Ted Lindsay Award.

In 2014-15, he finished with the highest points-per-game average of any player in the NHL, scoring both his 800th point and 500th goal during the season.

The 2015-16 season started woefully, where he had difficulty scoring any points at all, but when a head coaching change came to Pittsburgh, his season turned around, and he outscored all other players in the period from December 12, 2015 through the end of the season. He scored his first natural hat trick in five years, scored his 900th point, his 600th assistant and won the Stanley Cup for the second time. He also took home the Conn Smythe.

FUN FACTS:

1. In 2015, he was number 11 on a list of the 20 most hated players in the NHL, as voted by other NHL players.
2. In 2010, he signed the richest endorsement deal in NHL history with Reebok. He also has endorsement deals with Tim Horton's, Bell Telephone and Gatorade.
3. He won gold with Team Canada in the 2010 and 2014 Olympic Games, the 2015 World Championships, and the 2016 Canada Cup.
4. In 2016 he joined Wayne Gretzky and Bobby Orr as only the third player to win the Conn Smythe, the Hart Trophy and the World Cup MVP Award in the same year.

5. He won an Emmy for his part in the television program *There's No Place Like Home with Sidney Crosby.*

"The Captain" Stevie Y
- Steve Yzerman

Stephen Gregory Yzerman was born on May 9, 1965 in Cranbrook, British Columbia, Canada. He grew up in Nepean, Ontario, where he played junior hockey. He attracted the attention of pro scouts while he was playing center with the Peterborough Petes of the OHL.

He was selected in the 1983 NHL Entry Draft, making him the first draft pick by the Detroit Red Wings' new owners, Mike and Marian Illitch. He made such an impression at training camp that instead of being sent back to Peterborough to "season," he was brought up to the NHL club to play. He made his rookie debut for Detroit in 1983 at only 18 years old, the first 18-year-old to debut in the NHL since 1969. His record as the youngest NHL player was unbroken for 27 years. In his first year as a pro, Yzerman won the Calder Cup as rookie of the year.

The Red Wings were in a terrible slump when he joined, a period sometimes called the "Dead Wings" era. They were in need of a talented player with leadership potential, and they found both in young Yzerman. He was named team captain in the 1986-87 season, the youngest captain in the team's history. The very next season, he rewarded head coach Jacques Demers' faith by leading the Red Wings to their first division title in 23 years.

Yzerman had a strong 1988-89 campaign, winning the Lester B. Pearson Award and placing third in that year's scoring race, just behind Mario Lemieux and Wayne Gretzky. He took home the Hart Trophy as league MVP.

A coaching change in 1993 brought Scotty Bowman to Detroit, and Yzerman and Bowman led the Red Wings to the Stanley Cup finals in 1995 for the first time since 1966, where they were swept by the New Jersey Devils. Detroit returned to the Stanley Cup playoffs in 1996 after setting a new NHL record with 63 wins in a season.

In the 1997-98 season, Yzerman finally led his Wings to the Stanley Cup, the first in 42 years. During the cup celebrations, the team suffered a tragedy when a limousine carrying two players, Slava Fetisov and Vladimir Konstantinov, and a team masseur named Sergei Mnatsakov crashed due to a drunk driver. All three passengers were injured, with Konstantinov and Mnatsakov suffering debilitating head injuries. The season was dedicated to the three men, and when the Red Wings repeated as champions in 1998-99, Yzerman chose the wheelchair-bound Konstantinov to be the first person to whom he passed the Stanley Cup.

In 1999, Yzerman became the 11th player in NHL history to score 600 goals, and he took home the Frank J. Selke Award as best defensive forward. He made the NHL All-Star First Team in 2000.

Injuries began to plague Yzerman in the 2001-02 season. He suffered a recurring serious knee injury, and though he led his team in the 2002 playoffs, he was skating with a joint that was bone-on-bone. Despite the obvious pain that he was in, Yzerman led the Wings to their tenth franchise Stanley Cup, and this time, he presented the Cup first to Scotty Bowman, the coach who had arguably created him, and who had announced his retirement prior to the playoffs.

Yzerman's knee would become a source of constant trouble. He underwent multiple surgeries and missed the first 66 games of the 2002-03 season, but returned to play in February.

On May 1, 2004, Yzerman was hit in the face by a slapshot by Rhett Warrener of the Calgary Flames during a playoff game. He suffered a fractured orbital bone and damage to the eye which was corrected surgically. He missed the rest of the 2004 postseason and the 2004 World Cup of Hockey, during which his Canadian teammates refused to wear the number 19, Yzerman's number, out of respect for him.

The 2005-06 season would be Yzerman's last as a player. He reached eighth place in the NHL all-time scorers' records, but he was unable to continue play due to the horrible condition of his knee. He retired on July 3, 2006. *Sports Illustrated* honored him with a commemorative edition documenting his career.

On September 25, 2006, the Detroit Red Wings hired Yzerman as team vice president and an alternate governor. He remained in the front office at Detroit until 2010, when he joined the Tampa Bay Lightning as general manager. He won the General Manager of the Year Award in 2015, the first Lightning GM in history to ever receive that honor. He is still serving as the GM for the Lightning.

FUN FACTS:

1. Yzerman holds the NHL record as the longest-serving captain with a single team - 19 seasons, 20 years and 1,303 games.
2. He ranks second behind Gordie Howe in every offensive category in Red Wings history, except for assists, where he finished first.
3. He was named general manager of Team Canada for the 2010 and 2014 Olympics, when Canada won the gold medal.
4. When the Red Wings retired his number in 2007, they added the letter "C" to his banner.
5. He won a gold medal as a player with Team Canada in the 2002 Salt Lake City Olympics.

The Finnish Flash - Teemu Selanne

Teemu Ilmari Selanne was born on July 3, 1970 in Helsinki, Finland. He played junior hockey in the development program for Jokerit, a pro team in the Liiga. In 1992, he won the Aarne Honkavaara Trophy as top goal scorer in the league.

He joined the Winnipeg Jets in the NHL for the 1992-93 season, and he scored two assists in his NHL debut game. Only two nights later, he scored his first NHL goal. In his fifth game, he scored his first hat trick, giving him eleven goals in twelve games. He broke the NHL record for goals by a rookie that year, a feat that won him the Calder Cup and a berth on the First All-Star Team.

His scoring touch fell off a bit in his sophomore season, but in the 1993-94 season, he scored his 100th career goal in his 130th game. He split the lockout-scarred 1994-95 season between Jokerit and the Jets, and halfway through the 1995-96 season, he was traded to Anaheim. He finished the season with 108 points, and followed it with another 100-point season in 1996-97.

In 1998, he scored his 500th career point and was a

finalist for the Hart Trophy and the Lady Byng. He was the inaugural winner of the Rocket Richard Trophy in 1999.

He was traded again in 2001, going this time to the San Jose Sharks. He led the team in goals and points, but the Sharks fell out of the playoff race. Selanne moved to the Colorado Avalanche in 2003, and his season was his worst ever as he struggled with a nagging knee injury and repeated surgeries. He took the time granted by the 2004 lockout to rest and recuperate.

When the league opened for business again in the 2005-06 season, he signed with Anaheim, and in his return season with the Mighty Ducks, he scored his 1000th point. He was awarded the Bill Masterton Memorial Trophy at season's end.

During the 2006-07 season, he became the 36th player in NHL history to score 500 goals. He also played his 1000th game and led Anaheim in goals and points. He scored a hat trick and played in his 10th All-Star Game. He also became Anaheim's all-time playoff scoring leader and won the Stanley Cup.

In 2008-09, he played his 1,100th regular season game, his 100th playoff game, and became only the sixth European player to score 1,200 career points. In 2009-10, he scored his 600th goal, only the 18th player in NHL history to do so.

In 2011-12, despite his continuing knee trouble, he became the oldest NHL player to appear in all 82 regular season games. He retired after the 2014 playoffs.

FUN FACTS:

1. With Team Finland, Selanne has won four Olympic medals (three bronze, one silver) and two World Championship medals (silver and bronze). He was the oldest player to win a med in Olympic hockey at the 2014 Sochi Olympics.
2. His number, 8, was the first number retired by Anaheim.
3. A 2013 documentary about him, titled *Selanne*, appropriately enough, became the highest grossing documentary in Finnish cinematic history.
4. He is the highest-scoring Finnish player in NHL history.
5. He entered the World Rally Championship, a car race, in 1997 and 1998, racing under the name Teukka Salama.

The Uke - Terry Sawchuk

Terrance Gordon Sawchuk was born in Winnipeg, Manitoba, Canada on December 28, 1929. He was the son of Ukrainian immigrants, and his ethnic background gave rise to his nickname, "the Uke" or "Ukey". He was a talented youngster, and his early play was so remarkable that a scout for the Detroit Red Wings asked him to work out with the team when he was only 14 years old.

The Red Wings signed him to an amateur contract and sent him into the development system. He started with the Galt Red Wings (Ontario) in 1946, and he signed his first professional contract with the Red Wings in 1947. He played with the Omaha Knights of the USHL and the Indianapolis Capitals of the AHL, winning Rookie of the Year in both leagues.

He joined the Red Wings in the NHL in 1949, where he again won Rookie of the Year. He is the only player to ever win the best rookie accolade in all three professional leagues. By the end of his tenure with the Red Wings, he had backstopped them to three Stanley Cups in five years and won three Vezina Trophies for best goalie.

His personal troubles were beginning to manifest at this time. Coach Jack Adams ordered Sawchuk to lose weight before the 1951-52 season, and he dutifully dropped 40 pounds. Unfortunately, his personality also underwent a change, and he became depressed, anxious, insecure and withdrawn. He began a long struggle with alcohol and spent the rest of his life afflicted with crippling self-doubt.

He was traded to Boston in 1955 to make room for a younger goalie, a move that upset him greatly. His health began to fail, and in 1956, he contracted mononucleosis. He returned to the ice after only two weeks, and his play suffered considerably. His body was weak, his spirits were crushed, and by many accounts, he was close to a nervous breakdown.

He announced his retirement in 1957 and was promptly vilified by the press and his own team's front office as a quitter. He bounced from team to team for the rest of his career, ending in a miserable playoff showing for the New York Rangers.

In May 1970, Sawchuk was sharing a house with his teammate from the Rangers, Ron Stewart. The two men were out drinking and began arguing over expenses for the house they shared, and they got into a physical altercation. In the ensuing scuffle, Sawchuk fell onto Stewart's knee and suffered internal injuries. His gall bladder was removed in an emergency surgery, and a short while later another emergency operation was undertaken to repair a torn and bleeding liver. He gave a statement to the press stating that his injury had been an accident. On May 31, 1970, he died from a pulmonary embolism at the age of only 40. A grand jury was convened in Nassau County, but Stewart was exonerated and Sawchuk's death was deemed to be accidental, as he had stated.

In the course of his hockey career, Sawchuk suffered greatly, not just mentally but physically as well. He had three operations on his right elbow, an appendectomy, a fractured instep, collapsed lungs, ruptured discs in his back, and severed tendons in his hand. He sustained so many cuts in his face that he received over 400 stitches, including three in his eyeball, before he consented to wear a protective mask in 1962. Crouching in the net left him with lordosis and a permanent stoop that prevented him from sleeping for more than two hours at a time.

He was posthumously inducted into the Hockey Hall of Fame in 1971 and finished his career with 501 wins and 115 shutouts, a record that would not fall until Martin Brodeur came along in 2009. He won the Vezina four times and took the ultimate prize four times, as well.

FUN FACTS:

1. The Detroit Red Wings retired his number, 1, on March 6, 1994.
2. He was named Manitoba's Player of the Century.
3. He has been ranked in the top ten hockey players of all time (and number one among goaltenders) by *The Hockey News.*
4. When Sawchuk was an active player, there was no such thing as a back-up goalie. He played every single game, every single night.

5. In 2017, he was part of the first group of players to be named one of the 100 greatest players in NHL history.

"The Great One" - Wayne Gretzky

Wayne Gretzky has been called the greatest hockey player to ever live. When he retired from the league in 1999, he held 61 NHL records and a fistful of unbelievable stats and accomplishments. He played for twenty years, and in that time, he scored more goals and more assists than any other player in the history of the league. He was the only NHL player to ever score 200 points in a single season, and he did it four times. He is known as "The Great One" for good reason.

Wayne was born in Brantford, Ontario, in 1961, and he skated for the first time when he was two years old. When he was six years old, he started playing on a team comprised of ten-year-olds, and he was still the best player on the ice. His play was so impressive that he began to attract the attention of the press when he was still only ten.

He signed his first professional contract with the World Hockey Association (WHA) when he was seventeen years old. The contract was a personal services contract, different from a standard players' contract. He was unable to sign with the NHL, because the league's rules barred players younger than the age of 20 from being signed. He played for the Indianapolis Racers, and he was, as usual, a raving success. He only played with the WHA for one year, but in that year he was the third highest scorer in the league.

The WHA folded and several players, including Gretzky, were absorbed by the NHL. He ended up playing for the Edmonton Oilers, and his first season with the NHL was in 1979. He started setting records and collecting hardware right away, receiving the Hart Memorial Trophy as the League MVP in his first season. With Gretzky on the team, the Oilers went on to win the Stanley Cup in 1984, 1985, 1987 and 1988.

In 1988, he was part of a multi-player and multi-million-dollar transaction between the Edmonton Oilers and the Los Angeles Kings, and he was traded to L.A. Many Canadians felt that he had abandoned his homeland, and a member of the Canadian parliament even tried to ban the move. Nevertheless, he became a King, and his presence electrified the hitherto untapped California hockey audience. The draw that he had, and the impact of his popularity on fan interest in the game, helped California land two more NHL teams and encouraged the league to expand into the so-called "sun belt".

Gretzky went on to play for the St. Louis Blues and the New York Rangers. He retired from active play in 1999. He was inducted into the Hall of Fame that same year, which required the NHL to waive its rule stating that players had to be retired for three years before they could be given that honor. He was the tenth player in the history of the league to have the three-year rule waived. Shortly after his retirement, his number, 99, was retired league-wide in 2000. The retirement ceremony took place at the All-Star Game. His is the only number to be retired across the entire NHL.

FUN FACTS:

1. He had a successful international playing career, winning gold for Canada in the Canada Cup for three consecutive years.
2. He has never won an Olympic medal, but he was the final torchbearer at the 2010 Olympic Games in Vancouver.
3. In 2000, Gretzky became part-owner of the Phoenix Coyotes, and he began as head coach for the franchise in 2005.
4. The Wayne Gretzky 99 Award is given to the Most Valuable Player in the Ontario Hockey League playoffs.
5. He always tucked his jersey into the right side of his hockey pants. This was a habit he developed when he was a child, when his jersey was too big for him.

ICE CHIPS

Girls Play, Too - Women's Hockey

Women and girls have been playing hockey for just as long as boys and men. In fact, Lord Stanley (after whom the Stanley Cup was named) had a daughter named Isobel who played competitively. The first recorded women's hockey game took place in Barry, Ontario in 1892, according to the Canadian Hockey Association; others claim that the first game took place in Ottawa in 1889. In any case, women have been hitting the ice for a long, long time.

The first organized women's hockey games were initially played at a few Canadian colleges and universities. By the 1920s, collegiate women's hockey had spread throughout Canada and into the United States. The first women's ice hockey trophy was the Lady Meredith Cup, which was competed for in 1920 in the Quebec Ladies' Hockey Association. In 1921, professional women's hockey began in western Canada as an adjunct to the Pacific Coast Hockey Association.

World War II spelled the end of women's hockey for several decades. Interest in women's hockey resumed in the 1950s and 1960s, but there was no organized play for women until the 1980s, when intercollegiate play resumed in Canada. In the United States, women's hockey was finally recognized by the NCAA in 1993. On the international scene, the first Women's World Ice Hockey Championships took place in 1990, and women's hockey made its debut in the Winter Olympics in the 1998 Nagano Games. The first gold medal was won by Team USA.

The Canadian Women's Hockey League was created in 2007, and it currently has five teams, four in Canada and one in Boston.

In March 2015, the National Women's Hockey League was founded. There are four teams, all domiciled in the United States: the Boston Pride, the Buffalo Beauts, the Connecticut Whale and the New York Riveters. The first season's games were broadcast on ESPN, but currently the NWHL is only shown on YouTube and on Sling TV. The NWHL's championship trophy is the Isobel Cup, named after Lady Isobel Gathorne-Hardy, the daughter of Lord Stanley.

In 1992, Manon Rheaume became the first woman to play in the NHL. She tended goal for the Tampa Bay Lightning in an exhibition game against the St. Louis Blues. She only played one more exhibition game before her NHL career ended.

There have been other ladies to play professionally on men's teams. In 1993, Erin Whitten played in goal for the Toledo Storm of the ECHL. She played four games and recorded two wins. Shannon Szabados became the first woman to achieve a shutout in a men's professional game in 2015 for the Columbus Cottonmouths of the SPHL. She is still playing professional hockey for the Peoria Rivermen, also of the SPHL.

In 2003, Canadian Olympic star Hayley Wickenheiser played for Salamat in the Finnish Second Division, where she became the first woman to score a goal in men's professional hockey. She finished her season with one goal and three assists in twelve games.

FUN FACTS:

1. The longest college hockey game in NCAA history was played between the RPI Engineers women's hockey team and Quinnipiac on February 28, 2010. The game went into five overtimes before Laura Gersten scored the game-winning goal.
2. Tatum Evarts worked as a power skating instructor for a number of NHL teams throughout the 1970s and 1980s.
3. Lexi Peters appeared in the EA Sports NHL 12 video game. She was the first female ice hockey player to do so.
4. According to USA Hockey, the number of active female hockey players in the United States in 2005 was 52,469.
5. Team Canada has won the Olympic gold medal in women's hockey four consecutive times.

Open Ice - Minorities in Hockey

There is no disputing that hockey began as a monoethnic Canadian phenomenon. Even today, fully 93% of players are white. In the past, the game had a reputation for being racist an exclusive. Part of the trouble that minorities have encountered with getting involved in hockey is that the game is just so expensive; between the cost of equipment, ice time, travel and league fees, the game is primarily the purview of the well-to-do, and sadly, many minorities do not have the financial wherewithal to swing that kind of expenditure. There are also cultural barriers, especially with recent immigrants from the Third World, who much prefer the Beautiful Game (soccer/football) and think hockey is too violent.

This doesn't mean that there are no minorities in hockey, however. In 2016, there were 32 African-American or African-Canadian players in the NHL. There were also a number of indigenous American and Canadian players, as well as players from Middle Eastern backgrounds and Latino bloodlines.

The NHL currently requires all players to undergo diversity training, and the NHL in cooperation with

USA Hockey has created a program called "Hockey is for Everybody." The group, which first met in Boston in 1993 at the instigation of Commissioner Gary Bettman and USA Hockey's Dave Ogrean, is dedicated to bringing hockey to disadvantaged and minority children.

African-Americans/African-Canadians

The first professional hockey player of African descent was Herb Carnegie, who played in the minor leagues in Canada from 1944-1954. It is believed that racism kept him out of the NHL. The New York Rangers made him an offer, but only on the condition that he could be "tuned white". He never reached the top league.

The first African-Canadian player in the NHL was Willie O'Ree, who suited up for the Boston Bruins on January 18, 1958. He only played 45 games. His rise to the NHL was even more remarkable because he had suffered a terrible injury while he was playing in juniors, when he took a slapshot to the face and lost 95% of the vision in his right eye. He learned to compensate and continued to play. O'Ree became the head of the NHL Diversity Program, a post he has held for over 16 years.

The first African-American player in the NHL was Val James, who played from 1982-1987. He played for the Buffalo Sabres under Coach Scotty Bowman, and he also laced them up for the Toronto Maple Leafs. He retired due to injury, but it is said that the trauma he experienced from racism was so bad that it took him 10 years to even watch hockey again after his retirement. He is the subject of the book *Black Ice: The Val James Story*.

Some of the African-American and African-Canadian NHL players, past and present, are: Grant Fehr, Jerome Iginla, Mike Grier, Joel Ward, P.K. Subban, Wayne Simmonds, Dustin Byfuglien, Anson Carter and Evander Kane.

Asians in the NHL

The first Asian-Canadian to play in the NHL was Larry Kwong, who played one game for the New York Islanders in March 1948. In 2015, Andong Song became the first Chinese-born player to be drafted into the NHL. He was also signed by the New York Islanders.

Some of the prominent Asian-American and Asian-Canadian players in the NHL include Devin Setoguchi, Matthew Dumba and Brandon Yip.

Latinos in the NHL

The first Latino NHL player was Rick Chartraw, who was born in Caracas, Venezuela. He was drafted by the Montreal Canadiens in 1974 and went on to win five Stanley Cups before his long career ended in 1984.
Some of the NHL players of Latin American descent are Scott Gomez, Al Montoya, Bill Guerin and Raffi Torres.

Indigenous Players

The first indigenous NHL player was Fred Sasakamoose, who played with the Chicago Blackhawks from 1954 to 1960. He was born to the Cree Nation on the Ahtahkakoop Reserve in Canada, and after his retirement, he went on to serve as chief of his band for six years. He founded the Northern Indian Hockey League to encourage indigenous kids to take up hockey.

NHL players of Native or First Nations descent include Carey Price (Ulkatcho First Nation), Jordin Tootoo (Inuk), T. J. Oshie (Ojibwe), Sheldon Souray (Metis), Rene Bourque (Metis), Jordan Nolan (Ojibwe), Dwight King (Metis), Cody McCormick (Chippewa), Vernon Fiddler (Metis), Kyle Chipchura (Metis), Michael Ferland (Cree) and Jonathan Cheechoo (Cree).

Middle Eastern NHL Players

The first NHL player of Middle Eastern descent was Jon Hanna (Lebanese and Syrian). He played from 1958 to 1968 and retired after playing 198 games. The first Middle Eastern player to win the Stanley Cup was Justin Abdelkader (Jordanian) of the Detroit Red Wings, who hoisted the Cup in 2008.

Additional NHL players of Middle Eastern descent include Nazem Kadrii, Brandon Saad, Ramzi Abid and Ed Hatoum.

FUN FACTS:

1. The starting goalie for Team USA in women's hockey is Julie Chen.
2. Seth Jones was the first African-American player to be drafted in the first round of the 2013 NHL Entry Draft. He was selected by the Nashville Predators and currently plays for the Columbus Blue Jackets. His father is Ronald "Popeye" Jones of the NBA's Dallas Mavericks.
3. When Joel Ward scored the series winning goal that eliminated Boston from the playoffs in 2012, he was the subject of scathingly racist online attacks, primarily on Twitter.

Everyone Can Play - Para Ice Hockey

Para ice hockey, also known as sledge hockey or sled hockey, is one of the most popular paralympic sports today. It was first invented in Sweden in the 1960s by two men who wanted to keep playing hockey despite their physical disability. They created a contraption called a sledge, which is a metal frame with a seat and two skate blades. The frame is set high enough for a puck to pass beneath it without impediment.

The first sledge hockey competition took place in Europe in 1971, and since that time, the game has expanded to Canada, the United States, and Japan. The sport became an official event in the Paralympic Games in Lillehammer, Norway, in 1994. Appropriately enough, Sweden took the first gold medal.

The rules of sledge hockey are the same as those of regular hockey, with the additional prohibition of "teeing," or running into another player with the front edge of the sled. Because of the special angles encountered in the game, sledge hockey has its own style of stick. The sledge hockey stick has a curved blade like a regular hockey stick, but the end is equipped with teeth that can be used to propel players across the ice and to help them maneuver during the game. The bench area is covered with smooth plastic or ice to ensure that there is no damage to the sledge blades, and entry to the bench is flush with the ice so that players need no assistance coming and going. Sledge hockey is a full contact sport, just like "stand-up" hockey, and there are online videos of punishing hits that Paralympic athletes have delivered.

In the 2010 Paralympic Games in Vancouver, teams were allowed to include female players on their rosters. Despite this relaxation of the rules, no women participated in the Games that year.

Because of the different interpretations of the word "sledge" in different languages, the International Paralympic Committee officially changed the name of the sport to para ice hockey. The name change became effective on November 30, 2016, but because the season had already started, the full rebranding will not take place until the 2017-18 season.

There is an annual world championship in para ice hockey, overseen by the International Paralympic Committee. The first official world championship took place in Sweden in 1996, and unsurprisingly, the host country took home the gold medal.

FUN FACTS:

1. USA Warriors is a sledge hockey team composed of wounded veterans of the United States Armed Forces. They receive support from the NHL, USA Hockey, and the Washington Capitals.
2. Brad Bowden of Canada is considered by many to be the best sledge hockey player in the world. He is a two-time paralympic gold medalist.
3. Steve Cash, the goaltender for Team USA in the paralympic games, recorded a shutout in every game he played in the 2010 Paralympics. In honor of this performance, he was awarded the Best Male Athlete with a Disability award at the 2010 ESPY Awards.
4. Hockey Canada has an official sledge hockey page on YouTube.
5. The USA Hockey Sled Classic is an annual round-robin tournament. All of the teams in the tournament are affiliated with NHL clubs, and they wear NHL jerseys during play.

DON'T FORGET YOUR FREE BOOKS

**GET THEM FOR FREE ON
WWW.TRIVIABILL.COM**

MORE BOOKS BY BILL O'NEILL

I hope you enjoyed this book and learned something new. Please feel free to check out some of my previous books on Amazon.